Tag, You're It!

To Nicky –
Thanks for all you do for
youth!

Kathy Kimball Bah

TAG,
YOU'RE IT!

50 *Easy Ways to Connect*
with Young People

KATHLEEN KIMBALL-BAKER

A SEARCH INSTITUTE PUBLICATION

Search — Practical research
INSTITUTE — benefiting children
and youth

In memory of Blake James Rogers (1984–2002),
who was my friend.

● ● ● ● ●

Tag, You're It! 50 Easy Ways to Connect with Young People
Kathleen Kimball-Baker
Copyright © 2003 by Search Institute

Library of Congress Cataloging-in-Publication Data
Kimball-Baker, Kathleen, 1955–
    Tag, you're it! : 50 easy ways to connect with young people /
Kathleen Kimball-Baker.
        p.   cm.
    ISBN 1-57482-830-4
    1. Teenagers and adults. 2. Parent and teenager. 3. Teacher-student relationships. 4. Interpersonal relations in adolescence. 5. Adolescent psychology. I. Search Institute (Minneapolis, Minn.) II. Title.
HQ799.2.A3 K53 2002
305.235'5—dc21

                                                                    2002012362

10   9   8   7   6   5   4   3   2   1

Search Institute
615 First Avenue NE, Suite 125
Minneapolis, MN 55413
612-376-8955
800-888-7828
www.search-institute.org

Credits
Editor: Kathryn (Kay) L. Hong
Design: Percolator
Production: Rebecca Manfredini,
    Mary Ellen Buscher

Contents

• • • • •

Acknowledgments

I had a little idea that became this book. Sounds simple enough, but between the idea and the book came a boatload of sacrifice, support, and bleary eyes—other people's, that is. I'd like to acknowledge those people right here and now.

Search Institute's publishing team sprang me from my daily desk duties to draft parts of the book so that they could understand what the heck I was so excited about. They liked what they saw, encouraged me to finish it, and put up with a whole lot of my working "off-site." And ultimately, it got done.

Of course, Senior Editor Kay Hong's encouragement, questions and revisions, and support were especially appreciated. I may be her boss, but she is my editor—lucky for me.

A number of other colleagues made the book possible. I thank: Andy Munoz, for the green light; Julianne Schauer, for publishing assistance and glue; Jay Alexander, Lynette Ward, Nancy Tellett-Royce, Judy Taccogna, Art Sesma, and Gene Roehlkepartain, for reviewing the proposal; Sandy Longfellow and Brent Bolstrom, for research assistance; Becky Manfredini and Mary Ellen Buscher, for production and design direction; Terri Swanson, for way more than I can write here; Anthony Strangis, for reading and marketing; Jill Shannon, for sleuthing for stories; Carol Paschke, for primo promo; Paul Kirst, for helping sort out finances on the project; Stefanie Anderson, for running the numbers; and Karolyn Josephson, for PR.

My gratitude to these fine reviewers: Mary Ackerman, Brent Bolstrom, Kalisha Davis, Delroy Calhoun, Gabriel Calhoun, Chris Fisher, Jennifer Griffin-Wiesner, Colette Illarde, Martin Levin, Marc Mannes, Judy Puncochar, Terri Swanson, Katie Peffer, Beki Saito, Nicole Yohalem and Alicia Wilson of Forum for Youth Investment, Pascal Thomas, and Rick Trierweiler.

Because this book is about bringing a kind of magic into the lives of young people, I want to acknowledge the people who have been "wizards" in the lives of my children and many others—they provided much inspiration: Kristen Borges, Chris Fisher, Chris Haggedorn, Jennifer Holt, Kay Hong, Sally LeClaire Leider, Doug Meeker, Helene Perry, and Beki Saito.

I'm also grateful to these asset builders: Kent Eklund, my mentor; Glenn Housholder, Erika Ludke, and Annie Menendez, friends for life; and Mrs. Waggoner, who invited me to tea when I was 11. Of course, I'd be nowhere without Celia Kimball, Stella and Simon Cottrell, the nieces (Simone, Lauren, Alex, and Taylor), and the Bakers (Randy, Sean, Laura, Erik, and Peyton)—whose love keeps me steeped in asset #40.

You're **IT!**

Yes, you! Remember playing tag when you were a kid? Everyone was running around, and the person who was "it" had to chase and catch someone else and tag that person to be "it." Once you became "it," you knew just what to do, right? You had to *connect* with someone else.

That's what this book is about—connecting. But the kind of "tag" I'm talking about isn't just for little children and it doesn't involve running *away* from anyone; it's played by adults on behalf of young people, it's both fun and rewarding, and you can't lose—unless you don't play, and then everybody loses. Are you curious enough to read a little further?

Then consider yourself tagged!

What does it mean to be "it"?!

Let me explain what I mean.

If you're like me, most likely you're an everyday, average kind of person. Someone trying to make a living, enjoy life a little, keep things moving. Maybe you've got kids of your own. Maybe you don't. Doesn't matter. Because if you're like many of us, you're pretty sure the kids you know are good kids, no matter what fashion trends they follow or music they listen to.

But what about those *other* kids? You know, the ones on the next block, the ones you don't know, even the ones talking loudly outside the cinema or hanging out looking tough at the entrance to the mall—what about them? Do you look the other way when they look at you? Do you cross the street to avoid them? Do you lock the car door when they approach? What can be done about them, or for them, or with them? Lots of us have asked those questions.

There *are* answers out there. In fact, study after study in the fields of youth development and resilience has made it clear that the single most important thing that can make a positive difference in the life of a young person—in the lives of "your" kids *and* "those other kids"—is the presence of a caring adult. But here's the reality: Research shows that most young people don't have enough caring adults in their lives. Why is that? Why aren't more adults realizing and acting on the idea that, for at least one young person, they could really be "it"?

Could it be that we are *afraid* of those teens? That's what I was starting to wonder, and that is the question I asked one afternoon in 1998 when, as part of a magazine assignment, I cruised the Mall of America in Bloomington, Minnesota, interviewing young people and adults.

The Mall of America attracts a multihued lot of people, from international tourists to city and suburban teens looking for a place to hang out. I interviewed both adults and young people. I spoke with maintenance workers, grandparents, business executives, shoppers, Muslim youth, Christian teens, truants, security people, shopkeepers, youth with spiked hair and tattoos, clean-cut kids, youth chain smoking, mothers and fathers strolling with their toddlers.

What I learned that day changed me irrevocably.

The adults by and large said yes, adults are afraid of teens—the ones they *don't* know. But these same interviewees said they felt warm and protective about the teens with whom they had relationships—their grandchildren, their sons, their nieces, their stepchildren, their daughters. How strange that the feelings these adults had toward the teens they knew morphed into fear when it came to "other" teens. What was so different about the teens these adults didn't know that would cause them to be fearful? Negative media images? Their clothes, hair, facial expressions? Was it simple stranger anxiety? Or a sense that the young people wouldn't want them around anyway? The difference intrigued and troubled me.

But what ultimately inspired me to write this book—what surprised me and touched me—were the words spoken by the *teens* I interviewed.

- *"I need more adult friends in my life."*

- *"I don't understand why adults are afraid of me. Is it because of how I dress or look? I'm really a nice person if they'd just get to know me."*

- *"Why do adults cross to the other side of the street rather than walk near me? I wouldn't hurt anyone."*

- *"Why do adults frown at me? Why won't they even look me in the eye?"*

- *"I wish adults would just be my friend."*

When you're standing in a megamall with a 6-foot, 6-inch teenage boy dressed in what some people might consider gang attire and he tells you he needs, wants, and would welcome more caring adults in his life, it's hard to remain unmoved.

Echoes from the Research

What is equally compelling is the ever-growing body of research that supports what that young man told me.

The organization I work for, Search Institute, has been conducting research about youth for more than 40 years. We're a national nonprofit organization with a mission to advance the well-being of adolescents and children by generating knowledge about their development and promoting its use in everyday life. In pursuing this mission, we have accumulated powerful evidence that it is through relationships with caring adults that youth build the strengths, resilience, and skills they need to thrive as adults. Not just connections with relatives, but connections with many caring adults in the community.

Our surveys of hundreds of thousands of young people in North America have told us one thing loud and clear: They both **need** and **want** you in their lives. That's right—*you*. Neighbor, shopkeeper, bus driver, grocery bagger, bank teller, investor, student, cab driver, mechanic, librarian, executive, rock star, retiree, councilperson, golfer, clerk, journalist—everyone!

So we published this book to show you just how easy—and important—it is to connect with youth right now. It's time for you to become an *asset builder*. And that's what I mean by saying, "Tag, you're it!"

A WHAT? AN ASSET BUILDER?

An asset builder is someone who makes a positive difference in the life of a young person by doing good things with and for them—on purpose. When Search Institute uses the word "assets," we're not talking about money or property. We're talking about *human* capital, the kind of *developmental assets* that make people strong, resilient, and happy. Over the years, researchers have identified 40 *developmental assets* that pack tremendous power for youth, important things like support, empowerment, constructive use of time, and positive values. Think of them as "building blocks" for healthy growth, many of which young people experience through their positive relationships with adults. The more developmental assets young people tell us they experience, the more good choices they make—and the fewer risky activities they engage in. (Learn more about the developmental assets in the charts at the end of this book.)

What's more, our research has also shown us that most adults actually share a commitment[1] to raising healthy children, even kids who are not their own, according to a 2000 national poll of 1,425 American adults about their relationships with young people. But many adults doubt that they personally have what it takes to help a young person, especially if they aren't parents themselves. This gap between what people say they believe and what they do echoes the contra-diction I heard during my interviews in the Mall of America. The poll revealed that many caring adults just don't know how to go about engaging in young people's lives; they often worry that they'll tread on someone else's turf or they'll be rejected. I can hear refrains of fear in the poll's findings, fear that furthers the disconnection between youth and adults.

But we know, from our research, the research of others, and our own experiences, that each human being does have incredible capacity to make a difference in the lives of young people. We've seen and heard about it over and over again from the tens of thousands of people in more than 600 communities[2] who have given asset building a try.

- *A New York school bus driver knows every one of her riders by name.*

- *A mayor successfully campaigns for teenagers to become voting members on all city commissions and boards in Idaho.*

- *A fast-food restaurant manager in Michigan includes training on peer leadership as part of new-employee orientation.*

- *The Boys and Girls Clubs of British Columbia expand their focus beyond programs to emphasize asset-building relationships among young people and staff.*

Across North America and in a growing number of other countries, people are trying simple ways to connect with young people; some of the ideas in this book are inspired by their actions. If you choose to be an asset builder, you will definitely not be alone!

WHAT ARE THE REWARDS?

The research is compelling. But what's in it for you, you may be asking? Why should you bother to take the time and make the effort to get to know young people?

I can tell you why I did, and why it's been richly rewarding for me.

What appeals to me is this: asset building is about hope, about finding the goodness in people. While news reports may carry stories of despair and misery, asset building grounds me in what's right with the world. I like that I can work to build assets one on one, or I can join with others, and I can see results. Every single teen I've met has changed me in some way, always for the better. When I witness their vulnerability, I'm reminded of how far I've come in my own life. When I witness their strength during turbulent times, I'm reminded of how resilient the human spirit is, even when it's very young.

Young people have inspired me with their artistry, honesty, and flexibility. They've taught me about myself, made me laugh till I cried, introduced me to poetry, art, movies, comedians, and sports that I might never have found on my own. My friendships with young people have helped me experience in new ways what's been around for ages. Case in point: I've heard the songs from *West Side Story* for years; I know them by heart. But when I saw the musical performed by high school friends who had lived through the violent deaths of five of their peers in one year, the music resonated with meaning beyond anything I could have imagined. And it was as unforgettable for me as it was for everyone else in the standing-room-only auditorium: we were all moved to tears. That leads to me another reward I've experienced—connection to many, many others who put the same premium on valuing young people.

What's in it for *you* when you connect with young people depends on you. I'm going to assume that if you're reading this book, someone thinks you mattered enough to give it to you—someone cares about you. Or you picked the book up on your own out of curiosity about how to help young people; maybe your kind heart needs some company. If you decide to embark on building a relationship with a young person, for starters you can expect to experience fun, friendship, laughter, a renewed sense of wonder and purpose, and an improved sense of well-being. But the benefits are even bigger, especially if you join others in supporting teens. Building connections with young people and other caring adults also strengthens your community and builds a healthier future for all of us.

INTRIGUED, BUT NOT SURE YOU CAN REALLY MAKE A DIFFERENCE?

Then think back to your own childhood and ask yourself, who was there for you? Who made a difference for you? When we ask these questions at trainings and workshops, we find that almost everyone remembers at least one or two special adults whose attention, caring, and belief in them was very important in helping them recognize a talent, get through a tough time, or see things in a new way. Maybe it was a teacher, the one who told you the truth when no one else did or who challenged you to do your best when others were letting you slide. Maybe it was a neighbor who saw how much you liked his dog and who let you play with it and go on walks together. Maybe it was a teenager who took the time to play with you when you were small, who played her records and curled your hair and didn't dismiss you as just a little kid.

Are you thinking that those things don't sound very hard or very meaningful? Well, they *aren't* very hard to do; think how easy it would be for you, when you're outside working on the yard or waiting for the bus, to just say hello to the young people in the vicinity. You can introduce yourself, start slow, get to know one or two, and offer your friendship; you can start by using some of the ideas in this book.

These little things can be so meaningful to a young person. Want an example? You can find lots of them, in your own life, in your friends' lives, and probably in almost every autobiography ever written. But here's one to inspire you. Imagine a small, sensitive girl growing up in the southern United States in the early part of the century, amid poverty and prejudice. Her home life is unsettled, and she and her brother live at various times with their mother, grandmother, or father. The girl's relationship with her brother is one of the good things in her life, as is her love of reading. But when she is harmed and exploited by the mother's boyfriend, her life becomes almost unbearable; she stops talking, for the most part, and suffers silently through the days. Then, she says in her autobiography of that childhood, "I met, or rather got to know, the lady who threw me my first life line."

This "life line" was a thin, graceful, dignified neighbor named Mrs. Flowers, who one day invited the silent girl to her home for tea. She spoke to the girl about her love of reading, and told her that she knew she was having trouble in school because she wouldn't talk. So she had decided she would lend her books, including books of poetry, and ask that the little girl read aloud to her. Then they had tea, during which, incidentally, the girl learned some lessons of etiquette as well as experiencing the care and interest of a kind adult. How formative and important that "life line" was is apparent when you know that the sensitive, hurting child grew up to become a strong, successful woman who truly found and celebrated her voice—the poet Maya Angelou.[3]

Maybe not all your actions will be so dramatic or have such a lasting, deep effect on each child you encounter. But if you can still remember the small acts of a few special adults, be assured that young people nowadays will remember the gestures you make on their behalf. You may never know just which young person really benefits from your attention, but you'll have the satisfaction of reaching out and doing what you can, and you can trust the experiences of yourself and so many others that some of those simple actions are going to matter.

It's time for you to be that teacher, that neighbor, that older friend to one or more of today's young people. And we know you can do it!

HOW ABOUT THIS FOR A TRIAL RUN?

Scan the Table of Contents, pick one of the actions that catches your attention, then read it (the simpler ones are at the front). Each action is backed by solid numbers, research, or an expert opinion. If you're interested, but feel a little hesitation before you try something, check out the FSWs (frequently stated worries) on page 120 and the description of the developmental assets that begins on page 130. Then, give it a whirl. In fact, try out a couple of actions. After all, you might feel a little awkward at first, or catch a young person you want to connect with at a bad time or when he or she is preoccupied. (The way things are in our age-segregated society, the young person you approach at first may be so surprised that he or she won't say anything at all!) But persevere, try it a few more times, and it's likely you'll be successful in making a young person's day with your sincere interest and caring.

We're convinced that the more people who know about and act on their own power to build assets, the better off all young people will be—and ultimately the rest of us, too! So on your mark, get set, and go! Because . . . tag, you're it!

Notes

1. *Grading Grown-ups: American Adults Report on Their* Real *Relationships with Kids* is the result of a nationwide study of how adults think about their capacity, responsibility, and motivation for contributing to a young person's healthy development. It is based on a nationally representative telephone survey of 1,425 American adults conducted by the Gallup Organization. The study sought to determine whether—and to what extent—adults support and engage in 19 specific, asset-building actions with children and teenagers outside their own families. The complete report and report summary can be downloaded free of charge at www.search-institute.org.

2. Healthy Communities • Healthy Youth is a national initiative of Search Institute that seeks to motivate and equip individuals, organizations, and their leaders to join together in nurturing competent, caring, and responsible children and adolescents. The initiative sponsors research, evaluation, training, technical assistance, networking opportunities (including an annual national conference), and the development of resource materials based on Search Institute's framework of developmental assets. The initiative is supported by school districts, city agencies, community collaborations, state agencies, youth organizations, community foundations, corporate sponsors, and residents in hundreds of communities across the country. For more information, visit www.search-institute.org.

3. You can find the full story of Maya Angelou's "life line" in her autobiography *I Know Why the Caged Bird Sings,* first published in 1970.

Introduce Yourself

New to a neighborhood, apartment complex, or town?

Introduce yourself to one young person, parent, or adult a week. Even if you get a few strange looks at first, know that you're doing your part to make the area friendlier—for yourself, young people, their parents, anyone.

Or are you one of the settled, long-time residents of your neighborhood? Revive the old custom of welcoming newcomers with a kind word, an exchange of names, and perhaps even some home-baked cookies.

Added bonus: Neighbors who know each other can keep their neighborhood safer.

• • • • •

After analyzing studies on neighborhoods, families, and young people, a prominent sociologist concluded that families can do better at raising their children when they live in healthy communities, and one important element of a healthy community is a high level of connection among adult neighbors.

Schorr 1997

2

Be First to Smile

Many young people, especially when they reach adolescence, feel as if they become invisible to adults, or worse, are seen as the scourge of the earth.

Do you pay attention to the young people you come into contact with each day? Sure, you can't help but notice young people who are trying hard to be noticed. But what about the girl with the quiet gray sweatshirt walking by, toting a heavy backpack, or the boy with the cap pulled low on his blemished forehead sitting alone at a café?

They all need to be recognized and to feel important enough to be noticed. A smile is a small but real way to say, "You're important."

Remember when you were that age? It's no easier for them than it was for you. Remember what was on your mind back then? Most likely, you were plenty preoccupied with big questions about life and love, your looks, your future, whether you'd do well.

Next time you see a young person, any young person, don't look away. Catch his or her eye, and then offer up a little gift: your smile, a sign of your genuine goodwill. Chances are you'll receive a rather surprised grin in return. That was the experience of Terri Swanson, a colleague of mine at Search Institute, when she went on a jog through her neighborhood and smiled at and greeted the brother of a girl who babysat for her three kids. Although they had been neighbors for several years, Brandon and Terri hadn't really connected until that moment. He was a little surprised at first to be noticed, but since that day, they've gotten to know each other better.

Even if your first efforts meet with surprise, keep trying. Before long, it won't feel so awkward—and you'll have made the path you both are traveling a little easier.

• • • • •

Feelings of unconditional self-worth are achieved when people come to realize they are important and worthwhile regardless of performance or appearance.

Page 1992

3

Learn Their Names, and Use Them

Do you see "no-name" youth in your everyday life? Maybe they are waiting for a school bus when you're walking your dog. Hanging out in front of the convenience store as you fill your gas tank. Collecting the last run of interoffice mail. Bagging your groceries. Taking your movie ticket.

It's not hard to find out their names. Just ask—or notice their name badges. It's part of being civil, knowing names and using them. You don't have to insert their names into every sentence of your conversation. But certainly, it's easy enough to say, "Thank you, Carlos" or "Emily, can you tell me where I can find a phone?" or "How do you like your job, Vince?" or "Hi, my name is Mary. I always see you behind the register and I feel as if I should know *your* name, too!"

If you care to take it further, ask young people how they got their names. It's amazing how much you can learn about someone's cultural heritage and family history.

When Helene Perry of Minneapolis, Minnesota, taught

sixth grade, she used this idea as an icebreaker on back-to-school night, with a very diverse group of parents and students telling their naming stories while seated in a circle. She found that this simple act of sharing was a powerful way to foster connections, build understanding, and start new friendships faster.

• • • • •

The relationships and connections young people have with caring others are critical elements in their healthy development.

Scales and Leffert 1999

4

Look Out Your Window

There's a public service announcement that has run on Kansas television stations that tells an unforgettable story. And it's true.

It's the story of a youth who waited at the school bus stop in front of a house where an elderly woman lived. Every day, she stood at the front window of her house and watched as he got on. Maybe she waved or smiled once in a while, that's all. They had never actually spoken, but he knew she was watching, and it made him feel safe.

They never had a chance to meet, but to this day, he can't pass that house without thinking about the powerful, quiet presence of the woman who watched over him.

If you look out your window and often see a young person there alone or with a few friends, watch, and maybe wave or smile. You'll help them feel a part of the community. And if you see activities that don't look right, trust the instincts that will keep your neighborhood (including the young people) safe. Don't assume that the youth out there *want* to be in harm's way or have chosen to "make trouble."

Chances are they're scared—and at risk of becoming a victim. If stepping outside or even calling law enforcement will keep them safe, by all means do so. The old woman in Kansas would have.

• • • • •

In a study of two disadvantaged communities, residents agreed on some elements of an ideal neighborhood. They want safe places where children and adults can do things together, and they want to be surrounded by people who feel valued and who are involved in improving the neighborhood.

Saito, Sullivan, and Hintz 2000

5

Go to His Play

When schools feel a budget pinch, what's first to go? Creative activities, probably, like art, music, and theater. Sure, reading, writing, and math are essential. But not all young people find their success—or their calling—in these subjects.

Just as academically gifted youth need advanced classes to stretch their abilities, creative teens need "safe havens" to express and sharpen their imaginative, sometimes quirky talents. Without such opportunities, creative youth can feel out of place, not good enough, and at loose ends.

You've no doubt seen in print the names of the high school valedictorian or students on the honor roll. But when is the last time the local newspaper noted the student director who just staged a comedy by George Bernard Shaw? Or the young glassblower who just sold his first piece in a gallery? Or the young songwriter who just recorded her first CD? Or the woodworker whose first piece of fine furniture is on display in a local storefront? Creative youth need their gifts acknowledged and supported, too.

So show young people how much you value their creative pursuits, because those pursuits can really be important to their development and to their future. Check out what art events are offered by a nearby school, community center, or coffee shop. Then, attend a play, view the artwork, listen to the concert. In 20 years you might just look back and realize that you witnessed the early years of the next Gwyneth Paltrow or Pablo Picasso. You'll have given your creative pal a gift greater than a thousand words.

• • • • •

Studies show that young people's involvement in creative activities is associated with higher self-esteem, increased motivation, and higher achievement.

Scales and Leffert 1999

6

Ask for Help

Maybe you've stared at the flaking paint on your front door for years, thinking you'll scrape and repaint it one of these days. But still, it's not done. Or perhaps you've considered pulling weeds or picking up litter from the vacant lot eyesore down the street, but the task simply feels too big.

Anytime you feel stalled out, think *new* energy—young person energy. If teens are not doing much in your neighborhood, perhaps it's because nobody's asked. Consider this: What may be a burden to you could be an opportunity for school credit, a boost to self-esteem, even an escape from boredom for a young person.

When Rasheed Newson of Indianapolis was 19, he offered these wise words to a conference of asset builders: "One reason youth volunteer is because, at their best, volunteer opportunities allow youth to be in control, to make decisions. Unfortunately, the lives of youth don't allow them that kind of freedom. They go to school as they're told and shuffle from classroom to classroom at the sounding of the bell. How often does anyone go to them with major decisions and say, 'What do you think we should do?'"

Of course, paying whatever you can for their help or offering to do a favor in return is another way to show how much you value their assistance.

Give it a try. You'll be doing someone else—and yourself—a favor.

• • • • •

A Gallup poll found that adolescents were four times more likely to volunteer and help out in the community if they were asked than if they were not, but that only half of a national sample of 12- to 17-year-olds said that adults did, indeed, ask them to help out.

Hodgkinson and Weitzman 1996

7

Find Out When the Freshmen Play, and Go to a Game

Isn't it always the high school varsity team that gets all the attention? TV sportscasters chirp out its scores and newspapers report them the next day. Cheerleaders usually turn out in full force for the varsity games. And the stands are frequently well populated.

But ask a freshman (first-year) player or one on the junior varsity team just how many people came to the last game. Your young friend can probably tell you—because there were few enough to count on one or two hands.

In Georgetown, Texas, a group of older residents in a local retirement community decided to become asset builders for the young athletes in the area. They formed a booster group and now show up at local games. They enjoy the activities as much as the students do.

So how about asking for a game schedule? Put the dates on your calendar and try to attend at least one game or match this season. Even if you can't make the whole event, just show up. Plenty of youth don't have anyone in the stands or on the sidelines cheering them on, but they're out on the field or the court, trying their hardest to improve their performance.

Your being there is sure to sweeten the victory—or soften the loss. It might also be just what keeps them in the game.

● ● ● ● ●

Support provided by other adults, neighbors, and the neighborhood environment has been associated, directly or indirectly, with higher grades, higher school completion rates, less substance abuse, fewer feelings of loneliness, and greater self-esteem, hopes for the future, and cheerfulness.

Scales and Leffert 1999

8

Let Parents Know You Want to Be a Friend

Maybe you're just a little uncomfortable with the idea of getting to know a young person better before getting to know the parents or guardians better. Maybe you're worried they'll think you're a busybody or too pushy or just plain odd or that you're implying that they're doing a bad job.

Anything's possible. But more than likely, they'll be thrilled! Parenting, as you may know if you have kids of your own, is tough, tough work: no let-ups, very few breaks. Most parents would welcome more caring adults in the lives of their children and teens, someone else with whom their kids can share their victories, explore new ideas, learn new skills.

Some parents have the gumption to ask others to befriend their child. (I'm a parent who did and am so grateful the person I asked accepted!) If you do get asked, no special training is needed to follow through. Just be willing to be a friend now and then. But you don't have to wait for the invitation; ask. It may already be open, even if it's unspoken.

And trust me on this one: you'll get as much from this friendship as the young person will. Not to mention the parents!

● ● ● ● ●

According to the nonprofit research organization Public Agenda's survey of adults, half or more say they would be very comfortable complimenting a neighborhood child, watching a child while a neighbor runs an errand, taking a child to a ball game or show, or having a serious conversation about a problem.

Farkas and Johnson 1997

9

Set Limits Firmly—and Kindly

Places that feel safe, orderly, predictable yet not oppressive—
what some might call civil—don't just happen accidentally.
Nor do they stay that way automatically. They exist because
people care enough to do the work that makes them good
places to be.

Most young people breathe a sigh of relief when they
can be in civil surroundings. They know what's in-bounds
and what's out of bounds. They know what's accepted and
what's not. Things aren't chaotic.

The easiest place to create civil surroundings may be
right where you live. Perhaps you'd like to ban shouting or
keep the television off during meals so conversation can
happen. You can also expect your neighborhood to be civil
and take simple steps to make it so.

Randy Baker, a father in an urban neighborhood in
Minneapolis, Minnesota, for example, got fed up hearing
his unsupervised 15-year-old neighbor and buddies swearing
loudly as they played basketball. He walked across the street,
looked into their eyes, and simply but firmly told them that

he no longer wanted to hear such language on his block. The youth were quite apologetic, and they stopped. No lip, no retaliation, no harm done. Up till then, no one had set the limits. After that, Randy and the youth had plenty of pleasant exchanges, including an occasional game of hoops together.

So go ahead, set limits. Be clear, give reasons for the boundaries, and be sure that your limit setting shows caring and respect. It's the civil thing to do.

• • • • •

The presence of neighborhood boundaries is associated, directly or indirectly, with higher levels of achievement and high school graduation, decreased problem behaviors, and improved health behaviors for young people.

Scales and Leffert 1999

10

Notice and Act

When it comes to teens, too many people look away.

Kendra Youngren of Greeley, Colorado, when she was 16, put it this way: "Adults need to make more time for youth because more likely than not, youth are not going to be the ones to come forward. Adults have to seek them out."

So when adults actually do pay *attention* to young people and their world—the payback can seem almost like magic.

Think of how easy it really is. Next time you meet a young person on the sidewalk or in the mall hallway, don't look away. Engage in a simple act of noticing and meet her or his eyes with a friendly look.

Or say that you haven't seen your young neighbor for a few days. You might act on that noticing by just checking in with his folks; maybe you'll find out he just got an after-school job at a nearby hardware store. You've been meaning to pick up batteries for a week, so you stop by the store, say "hi" to your young neighbor, make your purchase, and put in a good word for him with the boss.

In one fell swoop, you do yourself a favor, bring business to your community, and make a statement that your friend matters to you and is valuable to others. Not bad for a little bit of attention.

• • • • •

An internationally recognized author, parent educator, and expert on human development and relationships suggests that being alert, noticing, and being responsive are activities that form part of the glue of connection with another person. People build connection with another by noticing their mood, accomplishments, behaviors, unspoken messages, and personal requests.

Clarke 1999

11

Shut Down a Stereotype

There was a time I got my kicks shocking other adults with the following words: "I have three teenagers right now—and I *love* it!"

It's not that the years with teens have been all smooth sailing. I've seen my children struggle with substance use and heard the screech of tires "peeling out" when they caught rides with fast-moving friends. I've searched at 3 A.M. for one curfew breaker, and had dinner with a brunette daughter, only to say goodnight to a bleached blonde.

What I've found fascinating are the changes that lead to growth in their lives—their opinions, their clothes, their looks, their likes, their passions, their moods, and their dreams. It's never boring. The experience of parenting teens reminds me of the wonder of watching children grow during their first year of life. The velocity of change and unfurling of the abilities and competencies are remarkable. I've learned more from two-minute chats with teens than from two-hour lectures by parenting experts.

Have you bought into the myth that the teen years are

necessarily heart-breaking? If so, imagine what teens must be anticipating. Try putting a whole new spin on adolescence. The next time you hear someone offer condolences to parents of a young person who's just turned 13, counter with *congratulations*. You may be rewarded with a look of shock, a perfect opening to bust a myth—and a chance to transform anxiety at least into curiosity.

• • • • •

Counter to stereotypes of adolescence as a period of stress and turmoil, research indicates that the majority of parents and adolescents adjust relatively well to this stage of development.

Stringer 1997

12

Judge Less, Support More

Is there a young person in your neighborhood, apartment building, or community who seems to have a reputation as a "troublemaker"? Something goes amiss—a broken window, broken bottles in the street—and everyone jumps right to the conclusion: Oh, it must've been *that* kid.

It's easy to go along with the suspicion. After all, she doesn't seem to have much supervision. Or he's always with a swarm of buddies, talking loudly and driving off at stock-car speeds. It's not unusual for adults to simply "write off" such a young person, to assume that he's headed for a life of trouble or that she's too far gone for ordinary people to help.

But even when young people do need professional help in their lives, they also need people just like you. So try switching gears. Ask yourself: does this young person have any friendly, supportive adults in her or his life? Imagine what it would be like to be the object of everyone's suspicions all the time. Then consider what a surprise it would be to have someone smile at you for a change, or greet you by name, or ask how things are going in your life.

You *will* stand out for this young person. When adults who've turned their lives around are asked what made a difference, it's often the kindness of a handful of people they remember.

• • • • •

All adolescents must find ways to earn respect, establish a sense of belonging, make close and enduring human relationships, and build a sense of personal worth based on useful skills. They must have the help of caring adults to develop a positive vision of the future, to see images of what adulthood offers and requires, and to prepare themselves for opportunities that are available to them.

Carnegie Council on Adolescent Development 1995

13

Hire a Young Person

Among North America's vast wealth of business resources, there is one that remains largely untapped today—young people.

Despite the fact that they virtually run the service economy on the weekends—checking you out at grocery stores, seating or serving you at restaurants, frothing your latté at the coffee shop, and tearing your ticket stubs at events—there is so much *more* that young people have to offer.

Robert Cline of Grand Rapids, Minnesota, spoke these words to a group of asset builders when he was 17: "What would it be like if we gave youth the opportunity to have a place in our society? The amount we can give is phenomenal. We are at our peak of creative ability when we are younger. We are also at our peak of risk-taking ability. If we were to hone these attributes of creativity and risk taking in this society, we could achieve so much."

So the next time you find yourself scratching your head over a vexing work problem, try asking a young person for a fresh take. It's entirely possible your next editorial writer, youth worker, math tutor, merchandising expert, graphic artist, software specialist, fundraiser, neighborhood revitalization consultant, Web designer, mechanic, or translator is younger than 18.

As you turn more to youth as resources, persevere even if a first experience doesn't work out as successfully as you'd hoped. You'll learn from it, and so will the young person you gave a chance to.

. . . . .

For youth who feel valued and useful, the research clearly shows many positive outcomes, including better mental health, high levels of moral reasoning, and more involvement in the community.

Scales and Leffert 1999

14

Do Something at a School

Like young people, schools need you. That's right—*you!*

Doesn't matter if you're a parent, either. No teaching experience is required. You don't even have to know a young person (though you will quickly get to know some if you do help).

If you can smile, use a telephone, stuff an envelope, blow up a balloon, pop corn, even stack a couple of folding chairs, you've got a skill a school can use. Can't get away during the day? Not a problem. Most schools have activities that need volunteers in the evenings. Or they can give you a list of people to recruit by phone for, say, field trip assistance or help with a big event. Typing lists is another big help.

Want to do a little more? How about volunteering to speak at career day, being a mentor for a service-learning project, working one-on-one with a young person who's struggling in a subject that came easily to you, or chaperoning a dance (most teens would much rather have *you* there than their parents!)? Bring along a friend if you're a little shy about going alone.

Janna Pathi, the only surgeon in Ohio County, Kentucky, stops by Wayland Alexander school every Wednesday morning to be a mentor. Since 1998, he's had to postpone only one mentoring session, and he speaks enthusiastically about the time he's spent playing chess, working on the computer, and talking about the future with a sixth-grade student named Curtis.

Call or stop by a nearby school and tell them you're willing to help out, even if it's in a small way. You may be surprised at how welcome—and appreciated—you'll be!

· · · · ·

Getting support from nonparent adults ("Other adult relationships") is one of the developmental assets associated with positive effects on students' school attendance, sense of bonding to school, effort, conduct, and performance.

Starkman, Scales, and Roberts 1999

15

Know the Curfew

Does your city, town, or county have a curfew for young people? Some do, some don't.

Whether or not you agree with the idea of curfews, make sure you know what time your young friends need to be off the streets for the evening. Curfews can vary based on age and day of the week or weekend. Find out for yourself what the curfews are—and help teens remember and abide by them. It's also important to ask your friends what curfew their families expect; these may in fact be more strict.

If you think your area needs new curfew laws or should change the ones it has, check in with any young people you know about them. Curfews could be an issue that inspires you and some young people to work on behalf of change in your community. Think about it: maybe what your community needs just as much are new teen centers, extracurricular programs like midnight basketball leagues, and more job opportunities for young people.

• • • • •

In a study of disadvantaged communities in Chicago and Denver, the higher the level of informal control in the neighborhood (defined as a general respect for authority and whether neighbors would respond if they saw someone in trouble or breaking the law), the higher the rates of youth involvement with peers who were not getting into trouble, and the lower the rates of youth problem behaviors.

Elliott et al. 1966

16

Speak Up

As you begin to see young people in a new light, you'll probably notice how widespread—and often wrong—negative stereotypes of teens are.

Challenge biases about young people when you hear them. When you speak from experience, your words hold power. People listen. You won't alter everyone's opinions, especially those who have had bad run-ins with young people. But you can offer another point of view.

You can also take things a step further. If you notice a store or business treating young people differently because they are teens, call them on it.

When my oldest child was 12, he asked me to take him to a gift shop to buy a present for his teacher. When we left the store, he told me that he'd noticed a clerk following him around, watching his every move from the corner of her eye. I immediately called the shop, pointed out the incident, and said I felt unwelcome in a store that treated my generally well-behaved son like a petty thief simply because he was wearing an oversized coat in which he *could* hide a shoplifted item. The clerk apologized and said she'd talk things over with the manager.

It's the same with stereotypes of youth as it is with stereotypes based on gender, skin color, ability, or any other characteristic: you work to change the actions based on stereotypes by noticing when they occur and speaking up about each incident.

One small action, one giant point, one person at a time, you can make a difference.

• • • • •

The majority of adolescents don't use drugs, fail in school, or engage in patterns of high-risk behaviors, although media coverage might lead many adults to believe the myths of "rotten kids and troubled adolescence."

Scales 2001

17

Lend Your Favorite Book and Borrow Hers

Martin Levin, a veteran of the publishing world, recently said: "A book is still the best value in the world—where else can you get 8 to 10 hours of entertainment for under $20?"

You can squeeze even more value from a book by sharing it with a young person.

It doesn't have to be a great classic; it doesn't even have to be mostly words. But when a book became one of your favorites when you were a young person, it's probably because the pages evoked something powerful in you: new ideas, laughter, a sense of not being alone, a change in your direction. The same is true for a young person today.

Dear Author: Students Write about the Books That Changed Their Lives is a collection of letters written by teens. It is packed with moving stories about how writers like Alex Haley, Helen Keller, Judy Blume, Arthur Ashe, and Lois Lowry helped young people come to terms with their disabilities, take pride in their ethnic heritage, cope with divorce, understand their own yearnings to grow, and shape their identity. After reading *The Autobiography of Malcolm X* by Alex Haley, 17-year-old Aslum Kahn of Rolling Meadows, Illinois, wrote: "You can't measure the amount of strength I got out of your book, Mr. Haley. It's something I feel even as I walk down the street. I realize now that I am a talented good person, and nobody can tell me otherwise."

Your favorite book will say a lot about you, as your young friend's favorite book can say a lot about her. If you're game, take it a step further: read special excerpts to each other and talk about why they mean something to you.

So open the door to a budding friendship with a young person by opening each other's favorite book.

· · · · ·

The use of reading materials to examine one's personality contributes to adjustment, growth, and development.

Beardsley 1982

18

Discuss the News

Earthquakes, elections, peace treaties, Supreme Court rulings, weird weather, athletic feats, and startling new scientific findings make great conversation openers with young people—and a possible call to action.

Even if they don't watch television news, listen to news radio, or read the newspaper, they're no doubt hearing news and probably talking about it at school, work, or home. On the other hand, some young people stay highly informed about the news, and may even excel more in "current events" than in traditional subjects but don't always have a way to show what they know.

So ask for an opinion and share yours. You never know where the conversation may lead—but new insights are a sure bet. And if you want to take another step, ask what the two of you might be able to contribute. Find out what causes you both find intriguing, alarming, or exciting, and explore the possibility of taking some kind of volunteer action together.

Taking action may not be the first thing you think of, and you may not know how to get started or what the most effective action might be. But it'll be fun and interesting to find out, and you're likely to find that it's meaningful to both of you when you succeed.

• • • • •

A Gallup survey found that one of the main reasons young people volunteered was their desire to do something about a cause that was important to them.

Hodgkinson and Weitzman 1996

19

Say What Makes You Happy

Ever had that all-hope-is-lost kind of moment, when you're just not sure you'll ever show your face in public again or you simply can't see your way out of a bad spell? Fortunately, the older we get, the more likely we are to believe the phrase: "This too will pass."

While some people are born optimists, others need extra help pulling out of bleak times. Many young people don't have the benefit of years of seeing how things improve given a few days, weeks, or months. Bad times can seem dire and permanent.

If your young friend's spirits plummet after a bad test, a fight with a friend, getting cut from a team, or enduring family strife, you can acknowledge his feelings and then be a reminder that not everything is gloomy. Even if he doesn't want to talk about what's troubling him or think of a silver lining to his current cloud, *you* can chat about something else. Let him see or hear about what helps you feel better, gives you joy, holds you spellbound, or makes you chuckle.

Taking an optimistic view can be learned, and you can help teach it by reminding your young friend to find ways to be happy, even when life looks grim.

• • • • •

A psychologist and clinical researcher who has been studying optimists and pessimists for decades says that cultivating a mature sense of optimism can enable a youth or adult to take charge, resist depression, feel better, and accomplish more.

Seligman 1998

20

Share Your
Favorite Music

For most of us, there's something about growing up that changes what music we like. You could call it a generation gap—or you can see it as a way to get to know a young person better.

Try swapping a CD or cassette tape with a young person you know. Listen to the music together if you can. But even if you listen separately, listen carefully—to the lyrics, to the overall messages, to the mix of instruments or voices.

Ask her which songs she ends up playing over and over again and what they make her think about. Tell her why you developed an interest in the music you picked. Talk about how songs may have helped you get through a tough time or captured the feelings that you couldn't put into words. Ask her if she's had a similar experience.

You might find that this music swap leads to a discussion of what each of you values—and that's great. Be as honest and open as possible.

The next time a young person drives by with loud music playing, you may hear something more than just the boom boom boom of the bass.

• • • • •

Perspective taking and seeing things from another's point of view is an important component of caring, probably through enhancing empathy.

Scales and Leffert 1999

21

Laugh

If you need a way to inject a little humor into your chats with a young person, trade tales of your most embarrassing moments and how you recovered from them.

Adolescents are likely to accumulate at least one incident a day they can tell you about. Sharing your stories can be an amusing way to build your bond. Or talk about your favorite funny movie, television show, or comedian.

There's nothing like a burst of good-natured laughter to take the sting out of an awkward moment—and put a little distance between the episode and the embarrassment. Talking about how you recovered from those moments and moved on can help a young person see that it will be possible to show his or her face again, no matter how bad the blunder.

• • • • •

By living with a humorous perspective, adults teach young people to manage life's challenges with less stress.
Sultanoff 1999

22

Expect Respect, and Show It, Too

You're human. You deserve respect. So does every young person out there.

Just like a boomerang, respect comes right back to you, especially if your aim is true. So help your young friend understand that respect cuts both ways. While it's certainly reasonable for you to expect respect, it's also important to model it. Try this: Be first to hold a door open, make friendly eye contact when you talk to a young person, speak politely, listen with true interest, model good manners. All easy things to do.

Young people can see a fake faster than an FBI agent can spot a bogus bill. So if you show *genuine* respect—and you expect it and earn it in return—you'll get it.

• • • • •

Expecting respect is a "social norm," according to findings of a 2001 Gallup poll of American adults; that is, of the 1,425 adults polled, a majority both believe expecting respect is important and act on that belief.
Scales, Benson, and Roehlkepartain 2001

23

Search Out What You Have in Common

You may think that you have nothing in common with a young person, much less something to talk about. Truth is, many of the issues are the same for young people now as they were for you—the struggle to understand yourself, the worries about "fitting in," the search for your purpose, the drive for independence, the ups and downs of family life, the power that friends exert, the need to be alone.

That's not to say that certain pressures haven't changed or that the world isn't different. But your journey through adolescence is no doubt full of memories and experiences that could help a young person see his or her own passage as possible. So try a talk with a young person about what's changed since you were a teen and what hasn't. And if you feel comfortable about it, share a real-life story.

My co-worker Kay was volunteering at a local children's home and became interested in a silent, isolated boy. She watched and waited to find whether they might have some common interest that would allow them to connect on a friendly, human basis.

Here's how she tells the story: "It was at the children's home's annual September festival that the interest appeared. When I arrived, feeling shy and nervous as I sometimes do around large groups of people, I headed for the sidelines where I had heard there'd be a 'zoo' with miniature horses, a llama, and baby goats. And there was Rob, holding the lead of a beautiful black miniature horse. He glanced at me but, typically, said nothing. I said 'Hi,' and focused my attention on the animals, then admitted out loud to Rob that I had gotten very nervous around the crowd and was so glad there were some animals here, because they made me feel more comfortable and safe.

"For the first time, after being acquainted for months, I saw Rob's face animated by an eager smile. And then he spoke! He said, 'Oh, do *you* feel that way, too?!' I said yes, and then asked about Rob's experience with the horses. He began to tell me all about them and how to care for them. And that new shared understanding and interest was the beginning of a friendship that we still have five years later."

● ● ● ● ●

To help adolescents learn what they must to survive and flourish, adults can work to understand what circumstances and challenges have changed. Such understanding can lead to strategies for helping young adolescents cope with a changing world.
Carnegie Council on Adolescent Development 1995

24

Listen

Here's a scenario you've probably encountered. You've had a really bad day and you just need to vent. You sit down with a friend, parent, husband, wife, brother, or sister—anyone willing to listen to your situation. You start talking, and no sooner do you set up the story, but your confidante jumps in with his or her own experience, suggestions, and advice.

The intentions were no doubt honorable, but what you really needed was someone to simply listen and understand. That's it. And that's often what a young person needs most, too.

A group of older asset builders in Denver know how to do this right. They visit local schools during lunch hours through a program called the "Listening Post" and let youth just talk about anything they want. The young people love it; sometimes there's standing room only around the Listening Post table.

If you like that idea, check in with a local school to see if they'd like to start a similar informal program. But you can also do this on the smaller scale of one-on-one. Just try to stay attuned to those times when your young friend needs you to keep quiet and let her talk. You'll know if you're invited to chime in because she'll ask. Or she'll pause and give you a quizzical look.

At that point you have a couple options. You could say, "Wow, that was tough" or "How did you handle it?" Or you might provide assurance that you have confidence in the young person's ability to get through it. But if you think she's looking for more from you, check in before you launch in. Ask: "Would you like me to give you some ideas or would you rather I just listen?" This may be one of those times when the best gift is careful listening.

• • • • •

In his book on getting along with others, a writer, speaker, and consultant about relationship skills says that listening carefully indicates that we care enough to understand our friends, to know who they are, what they think, and how they feel.

Hipp 1991

25

Compliment the Parents

Job available: Position includes 24-four hour shifts, seven days a week. Performance review may occur only after 21 years of service, through feedback available in the form of nasty looks in grocery store lines or the "cold shoulder" from a neighbor. Salary: none.

Job title: *parent.* You get the picture—help wanted. And how can you help? A simple way is to give parents a sincere word or two of praise about their child.

If you see a young person walk the dog, be kind to a child, pick up trash, carry in a bag of groceries—anything little or big—or if a friendship with the child is an important day brightener for you, by all means, let parents know. Say something like: "Well, you sure seem to be doing something right. I saw Julie . . ." or "I sure like Jamie. He always smiles at me and it really makes my day."

That one compliment could get a parent through days, even weeks of tough times, and remind the parent of one of her or his child's strengths or great qualities—not to mention the potential positive effects if the compliment is also passed along to the young person.

• • • • •

Parents can find new motivation in the idea of identifying and building on the strengths of their children and families, a technique considered one of the elements of effective youth and family programs.

Saito, Sullivan, and Hintz 2000

26

Point Out the Long View—and Take It, Too

The rare young person seems like an "old soul," an individual with a wisdom, intuition, and foresight beyond his years. But most are living right here and now, feeling each moment of the day intensely and struggling to make sense of a life that's just beginning to be lived.

Try to be patient if your young friends aren't yet connecting what they do today with what they can or can't do tomorrow. As obvious as it is to you, they might not yet grasp how a good grade on tomorrow's test will add to their overall grade point average in three weeks, raise their class rank at the end of the year, and help them go to college. Most teens will make the leap in judgment at some point— and you can help by taking the long view yourself.

If you remember when the light went on for you about consequences and the connection between today and tomorrow, by all means share that story. If your friend can see how you made it and how you learned to take the longer view, he or she just might be able to make the connection sooner.

In the meantime, if he messes up on a test because he didn't study, point him to his next chance. If she stays out too late one night, oversleeps, and misses her job interview, encourage her to call and reschedule. Keep your own irritation in check as long as possible and keep steering each young person forward—toward the long view.

• • • • •

Adolescents' expectations about their future lives, whether educational attainment, work, or family life, are influenced by adults whom young people perceive as "like them" or whom they wish to "be like."

Scales and Leffert 1999

27

Talk about People You Admire and Why

Whether it's your big sister, a firefighter, your dad, or your 9th-grade English teacher, the people you admire say a lot about what matters to you, what you value, and who has shaped your life.

Jot down the names of three people you admire and why. Try to pick people from different times in your life. Ask your young friend to do the same. Then share who you picked and why. Here are some ideas to consider in your conversation:

- *What qualities stand out in each person?*

- *When you look at the three different people, is it the same or different qualities that you admire in each?*

- *Have you aspired to be like any of these people?*

- *Have you changed in some way because of them?*

- *Have any of these people ever disappointed you? And how did you get past the disappointment?*

As you become better acquainted with your friend, you might be surprised to find you *both* become role models to each other.

• • • • •

Everyone needs heroes, whether they are famous people or our next door neighbor, to help them grow and define who they are.

Kraehmer 1995

28

Help Him Move through Frustrations

Your friend has argued with his mother, father, or sibling. He's fuming mad, convinced that his parents are completely unfair or his brother is impossible to live with.

In extreme cases, this may be true. But more than likely your friend will make peace again with family members pretty soon. Even if that peace is short-lived and he's miffed again the next day, each effort to resolve the conflict builds his skills and helps him see beyond today.

How can you help? Simple: just listen. Let your friend express himself until he starts to wind down. Try to be understanding, without necessarily taking sides. Then gently assure him that you believe he has what it takes to make it through this crisis. If he seems receptive, offer what wisdom and perspective you can and share what's worked for you in patching things up with family and friends. Or remind him that if the same strategies keep getting the same bad results, it might be time to try something new. Lighten up the mood, if you can, with a story about the silliest thing you ever got mad about.

Be available to your young friend—and help him move on.

• • • • •

As adolescents do what it takes to establish their own identity, separate from their parents, they often have vexing times with family members, especially mothers and fathers. Over all, though, research indicates that relationships between teens and parents become more cooperative during late adolescence.

Stringer 1997

29

Grow Something

Even a small patch of soil tucked between two high-rises can yield some impressive tomatoes, green beans, and lettuce.

As a way to spend time together, you and your young friend could till, plant, and tend a garden patch or create a container garden with potted plants. Seeds aren't expensive, sunshine and rain are free, and what you'll harvest from spending time together on nourishing living things will last far longer than the perishables you'll be putting on your tables.

And if you've never grown anything before, this could be a chance to learn something new together. You'll also get the benefit of a little exercise.

Your efforts could lead to bigger and better things, too. Want some inspiration? Try reading *Seedfolks,* by Paul Fleischman, either alone or together with your friend. In this lovely book for ages 10 and up, thirteen voices tell the story of the transformation of a trash-filled vacant lot in inner-city Cleveland into a neighborhood garden cultivated by a diverse group of nearby residents: old, young, female and male, Haitian, Korean, Hispanic, White, tough, lonely, hopeful. Together, they grow flowers and vegetables and at the same time nurture the young tendrils of a sense of community.

• • • • •

A well-known Stanford University scholar who has written extensively about the moral development of young people says both adults and young people learn and grow when they engage in a dialogue or project of mutual interest. He calls this intergenerational activity "respectful engagement."

Damon 1988

30

Play Games

Playing games can be more than recreation, especially if they make you use your brain. And if you're someone who's getting up in years, playing mentally challenging games can help you preserve your memory.

So see if your young friend can come out and play with *you*. You can pick up used board or card games at thrift stores or garage sales or visit your local park or community center to see what's available there. (In Portland, Oregon, a group of asset-building students and teachers created a "lending library" of games, puzzles, and activities when they saw how much fellow students got from spending time with adults playing games!)

Share what you know, including good strategies, and see if your friend can give you a few hints or introduce you to some games you haven't tried before.

You'll quickly discover each other's strengths—ability to improvise, to problem solve, to think ahead, to be creative. Be sure to compliment your friend when you observe these qualities.

Need a few recommendations? Some games that will test your wits, sharpen your thinking skills, and provide hours of amusement include riddles, chess, cribbage, dominoes, Scrabble, and Mad Libs.

• • • • •

In their five-year study of how adolescents prepare for adulthood, a psychologist and sociologist team found that when an activity is seen as like both work and play, young people tend to find the experience positive, feel good about themselves, and feel sociable, relaxed, and challenged.

Csikszentmihalyi and Schneider 2000

31

Walk Around—for a Change

Want a real eye-opening experience? Ask a young person to show you around—on foot—in your neighborhood. Even if you have traveled the same streets by car or bus for years, everything will look different if you see it through the eyes of your young friend.

What's the mood? Do people avoid eye contact or do they greet the two of you and smile? Where teens are gathered, are caring adults interacting with them? Are some youth clustered in front of a store or gas station, bored and restless? Can your friend point out places that truly welcome young people, feel safe, fun, respectful, and relaxed?

How accessible are places? Can a young person who doesn't drive or own a bike easily pick up school supplies, borrow a book, get to work, go with friends for a soda, or get to a public building holding a hearing on matters that affect youth? Can a young person on crutches or in a wheelchair access these same things?

Almost every neighborhood or community can use a little help. You and your friend may be the first to "see" what needs work. Take a small step together to make a change. Pick up litter as you walk, or send a letter—signed by both of you—to the newspaper or city council about repairing the play equipment in the local park. Audio- or videotape as you walk and send the tape to a radio or television station. Or each of you tell one other person what you found, invite them over for a chat, and see what the power of four can cook up and do.

• • • • •

Among the most powerful means of enriching young lives is to enlist their energies in improving their own communities. Young adolescents can and want to contribute to their communities, and they learn much from such engagement.
Carnegie Council on Adolescent Development 1995

32

Send Them Back to School

Ever been on your way to work, the grocery store, or community center and noticed a group of young people you recognize heading *away* from school rather than toward the building?

Do them a favor: if you know them, consider telling them to go back to school. Really. Try phrasing it in a mildly humorous or at least neutral way: "Hey, did my watch stop or is it time for school?" or "Hi, don't mean to be nosy, but shouldn't you be in school today?" My favorite phrase that almost always works is: "Hey, isn't school in the *other* direction?"

They may be quite surprised to hear you say something; most adults would just look the other way. And *you* may be surprised to see them actually turn around and head for school. If they argue with you or even mouth off, then leave well enough alone. Don't take it personally; you've made your point. A gentle reminder that neighbors are looking out for young people sends the message that people do care and they are important enough to merit your attention.

They may or may not turn back, but they're likely to think twice about skipping school again.

• • • • •

In a review of scientific studies on sources of support, researchers have found that while most youth prefer parents and peers as sources of support, on some issues, such as school concerns, nonparent adults often are preferred sources of advice.

Scales and Gibbons 1996

33

Send a Card

Let's say you've gotten to know a couple of young people in your building, on your block, or down the road a bit. As you're heading out the door one morning, you remember that this is the big day she's taking an important exam, or he's acting in his first play, or your young friend is going for an interview for an after-school job.

There's no time like the present to acknowledge her or him with a card, either by snail mail or e-mail. Nothing fancy. Just a note that says, "Hey, I hope things went well today! Be sure to let me know. You're great and I know you'll be a success!"

Or maybe you noticed that the young clerk at a store you frequent was especially competent and polite. How about taking 5 minutes to send a card to that clerk's boss or fill out an employee comment card? You'll let the boss know that her or his commitment to hiring young people is worthwhile.

Want to take this to the next level and multiply the good effects? Consider Anna Johnson's example. When this

Tennessee woman was a young worker almost 30 years ago, her employer received a letter from a customer who complimented Anna's work; he shared the letter at a staff meeting. The letter arrived at a time in Johnson's life when she desperately needed a boost, and she never forgot that incident. A couple years ago, she put the memory into practice with her own program to give other people a similar boost. She lines up a sponsor, purchases stamps, stationery, and envelopes, and sets up shop at a table in a mall, where she offers free delivery to anyone of any age who wants to send an encouraging letter. Last year she received $500 from her sponsor and sent 1,148 letters of encouragement!

• • • • •

In one study of 300 middle school students, the ones who had social support from "special adults" were also the ones who had the highest self-worth, most positive hopes for the future, and the most cheerfulness.

Talmi and Harter 1999

34

Say What You Value

This may come as a shock, but in a society that prizes its freedom to disagree on everything from ballots to body piercing, most adults actually *do* agree on some ideas about youth, according to a national poll of American adults conducted by the Gallup Organization in 2000. For example, the poll found that nearly three-quarters of those polled believe adults should discuss *personal* values with children and youth—values like honesty, integrity, and responsibility.

Of course, a lecture is probably not the answer. And your actions will speak more boldly than any opinion you express.

The main point is that you don't have to shy away from *voicing* what you value when you interact with young people. Allowing them a glimpse into how you grapple with tough questions and make your choices can give them the courage of their own convictions. After all, they're curious—and they're shoring up their own set of values.

Example: When singer and civil rights activist Joan Baez was 16, she became close friends with an older man named

Ira who attended the same Quaker meetinghouse and discussed with her his beliefs about nonviolence. She even invited him to speak to her high school English class. Ira told Joan's father that he saw in Joan "something extraordinary," and he was right. Her friendship with Ira helped shape the beliefs that led to her activism and vocal artistry protesting injustice.

• • • • •

In a 2000 Gallup poll, 73 percent of American adults said it is highly important for adults to "openly discuss their own values with children and youth." Through such discussions, young people are helped to learn how to shape their own values and beliefs in a complex world.

Scales, Benson, and Roehlkepartain 2001

35

Talk about Getting through Hard Times

Revealing mistakes you've made, "failures" you've lived through, regrets you have, or things you'd change if you could roll back time, is as important as—and sometimes even more valuable than—any pep talk you give a young person.

First, it shows you're human, not just "adult." Second, it gives young people a glimpse of the long view, as in the old saying, "life goes on."

One of my co-workers has found that revealing to young people her own struggles and mistakes as a teen can go a long way to creating trust and understanding between them. When Rachel, one of the teenage girls at a coffee shop she frequents, entrusted her with the information that her new boyfriend was pressuring her to have sex, my co-worker didn't lecture or use scare tactics. Instead, she told Rachel with honesty about some instances in her own teenage years when she herself gave in to such pressures, what the difficult consequences were, and what she did to get through those rough times to better times. Then she told Rachel how much potential she had for avoiding the same mistakes and living a wonderful life if only she is careful and makes good choices now. It was clear that Rachel took what was said more seriously because of my co-worker's self-revelation.

So go out on a limb. Tell your young friend how messing up your grade point average in high school or college took you out of the running for your dream job but helped you slow down your partying days. Or share how the time you got fired from one job made you feel like a lower life form but steered you in a direction that makes you much happier now. Or admit how you racked up $10,000 in credit card debt that took five years to recover from and persuaded you to try your best to live within your means.

Whatever your story, you might be sparing a young person a few lost years—and giving yourself a little break in the process.

• • • • •

The ability to deal constructively with disappointments and to learn from mistakes is linked to the development of emotional health. The ability to rebound from setbacks is a valuable inner resource.

Stringer 1997

36

Agree to Disagree

You've no doubt heard or used this line yourself: "Hey, it's a free country. I can say anything I want."

Practically from the time toddlers learn to speak, they seem to know and flaunt their right to free speech. But how well have we learned by the time we're adults to disagree in a constructive way? If you have, count yourself lucky. Unfortunately, too many others are either keeping their opinions to themselves to avoid conflict or shouting at the top of their voices to make sure they're heard over the other loud opinions.

There is something between the two extremes, and you can help your young friend learn how to argue effectively by first *agreeing* to disagree. If you acknowledge this early on in your friendship, you'll set the stage for being able to resolve things later. You won't have the same opinions about everything that you discuss or do together. That's good, because you can learn from each other.

When conflict arises, remind your friend of your agreement to disagree. Call a brief time-out if discussions get too heated, but come back to them if you can in an hour or a few days. Pushing through the conflict will only make your friendship stronger. And that's true for all your relationships—at home, work, or play.

• • • • •

"Perceiving conflict as opening up possibilities for improving a relationship encourages constructive behavior."

Weeks 1994

37

Talk about Money

In a society of corporations and entrepreneurs, most adults are remarkably reserved when it comes to talking personal finances. Parents often try to shield their children from the harsh reality of money woes or tight budgets. Or, if they can, they may try to make things easier for their kids by providing them with a generous allowance. But young people use money every day, and they need help in learning how to handle it wisely.

After all, the instant a teen comes of age—and often before that—credit card companies are sending them personalized mailings, extolling the virtues of their services. What young people need is a little balance in the face of this onslaught of "easy" money. Trustworthy, first-hand information, stories, and advice about the importance of and ways to earn, save, and share money can be hard to come by.

So whether you've made a fortune or just figured out how to stay afloat, you can be a priceless resource to your friend. Talk about the satisfaction of earning your first paycheck. Reveal budget mistakes you've made and any regrets you have, as well as your successes. Share stories of how you've gotten through touch-and-go times and how you feel about earning the money you spend. If you've received government assistance, explain how the system works and what you've learned. If you've figured out how to invest well, tell how you got to that point. If you donate to charity, discuss how you choose who gets your contributions.

• • • • •

Teaching youth about money not only improves their financial literacy, it enhances their knowledge about the connection between money and values.

Godfrey 1995

38

Tell What Makes Life Meaningful to You

Something gets you up and out the door each day, right? Whether it's your garden, a sports event, the need to put food on the table, a visit with a friend, responding to a hungry cat, or a chance to spend time out in nature, most of us find some way to plug meaning into our daily lives. But when you're 12, 15, or 18, it's not unusual to wonder what on earth all this homework, table waiting, standardized testing, or filling out of applications is actually going to get you.

So give a young person a glimpse of what makes life meaningful for you, and find out what's meaningful to her. All you have to do is be yourself and simply reveal one of your unique interests.

I often sit at my dining room table making beaded jewelry. It's a way to relax, reflect, and express my creative side. But perhaps the most rewarding part is that it has also become a way to connect with many young people (friends of my children) who've sat down to inspect what I'm doing.

I've had many wonderful conversations that began with: "Why do you bead?" We've chatted about ways to cope with stress, curfews, fights with parents, siblings, and friends. We've talked about our ethnic backgrounds (my Mexican grandparents were expert needleworkers), our favorite music, teachers, and foods. We've even discussed spiritual topics. Tenzin, a Tibetan teen, told me his beliefs about reincarnation in the same conversation he talked about how meaningful skateboarding had become for him since moving to Minnesota from halfway around the world.

You actually may have more in common than you think with your friend—and it sure doesn't hurt to remind yourself from time to time what makes it all worthwhile. Chances are your young friend is part of that.

• • • • •

Nearly three quarters of American adults believe it is important for adults to have conversations with young people that help adults and young people "really get to know one another."

Scales, Benson, and Roehlkepartain 2001

39

Go to the Polls Together

You've heard it for years—it's your privilege and responsibility to vote.

No doubt about it, casting a ballot for candidates who support your views of young people is critical. It's equally important that young people see you voting. By taking a young person with you to the polls, you'll show him the power he will ultimately wield as a responsible citizen. He'll also be seen by other adults, the ones who are voting and thereby making decisions that affect the young people's future.

You don't have to stop there, though; you can also show your friend other ways to "vote." Set a good example and make your preferences—and power—known with your feet, your phone, and your funds:

- *Show up where it matters—at school board meetings, at public hearings, at rallies.*

- *When candidates knock on your door, quiz them about issues important to teens.*

• Together, call, write, or e-mail your elected officials to express your opinions. Let them know you and your friend are paying attention to how they support young people.

• Every time you take out your checkbook or wallet, consider spending your money only at businesses that include and respect young people in hiring, serving, and making decisions.

• • • • •

Young people agree that good citizenship includes the obligation to vote, and students with the most civic knowledge are most likely to be open to participate in civic activities, according to an international survey of 14-year-olds.

Torney-Purta et al. 2001

40

Practice with Them

Know how to change a tire, hem a pair of pants, fix a leaky faucet, balance a checkbook, or fire up a barbecue? Pass on the skill! While these tasks may be easy, commonplace, or "no-brainers" to you, they may well seem Herculean to a young person.

Teens are like adults in training. Schools educate them in many ways, but certainly not in all ways. And parents may be too busy putting food on the table or paying the rent to even realize that they need to pass along some of these skills to their children.

The next time you plan to do some repairs on a car, fix an appliance, light some coals, or stitch a patch on a favorite pair of jeans, invite your young friend—girl *or* boy—to observe and help you. The more real-life skills they build, the more confidence they can have as they journey to adulthood.

Besides, it's often easier for some young people to talk when they are beside you rather than face to face. So you may find that working together on fixing something makes a great backdrop for an important conversation.

For a different twist on this idea, consider asking a young person to teach you something—how to make a Web home page? How to in-line skate? That kind of learning keeps you young while strengthening the foundation of your relationship with your young friend.

∙ ∙ ∙ ∙ ∙

An essential ingredient for growing up with sensible attitudes toward work is the availability of adult models who can teach by example what a young person needs to do to become a productive member of society.

Csikszentmihalyi and Schneider 2000

41

Walk Your Talk

The best way to express what you value is to *show* what you value.

One of the many benefits of getting to know a young person is that you can keep each other honest. You can start small with a simple commitment to follow through. If you say you'll show up, you show up and on time. If you offer or agree to help, you do it. Building up trust at the beginning of a relationship (with anyone, young or old) is so important that it's worth any extra effort it might require from you.

If you want to take it a step further, after talking about what each of you values, why not make a pact with your young friend to act on your beliefs, encourage each other, and tell each other what you did. If you share a commitment to something, say, working on the problem of hunger, you could do a mini-food drive together, then take your collection to a food shelf.

Of course, when you put your beliefs on the line, not only will young people listen, they'll also be watching.

They'll catch any inconsistency between your words and your actions faster than you can say, "But I'm only human." You *are* human, after all, as is your young friend, and walking your talk just may include a little forgive and forget.

• • • • •

In a survey of American adults, more than 70% agreed that children and youth needed to learn from adults such core shared values as equality, honesty, and responsibility.

Scales, Benson, and Roehlkepartain 2001

42

Meet Their Friends

Once you've built a friendship with a young person or two, get to know their friends, one by one.

They need as many caring adults in their lives as they can get, too. You'll be multiplying the power of your friendship, not to mention adding a lot more energy, humor, and insight to your life.

Learn their names, make them feel welcome, then take a step toward getting to know them. If you're a parent, how about inviting your middle-school child's friends to an early before-school pancake breakfast? If you're a neighbor, how about trying to show some interest in young people on their way home from school by handing each one a fresh-cut flower from your garden or inviting them to play fetch with your dog? Those are the kinds of situations when a group of young people fulfills the motto, "The more the merrier!"

If you give it a little thought and consider the ages, cultures, and interests of the young people involved, you'll be able to think of many more such situations.

• • • • •

In a groundbreaking book of 1998 on adolescents as a group isolated by and from most adults, the author writes: "We have to reconnect the adolescent community to ours. It is not so hard. We just need to reach out and embrace them and take the time to get to know them—one by one, as individuals."

Hersch 1998

43

Trust Her

Trust can be like a savings account. The more you put in, the more you get back.

But when a young person messes up, especially with a parent, she can feel downright bankrupt in the trust department. And it may seem like an eternity before she builds trust back up to a comfortable level.

While she's working to restore trust at home, stand by your young friend. Tell her that you believe she has the ability to put things right and to make good choices (because she does!). She'll treasure your reassurance more than you can imagine—and she'll come through.

One idea is to offer your young friend the opportunity to earn some trust in a brand new arena.

When my daughter, Laura, was 15 and we were struggling with curfew problems, I couldn't trust her to come home when she said she would and so her activities were more restricted. Beki Saito, a colleague then at Search Institute, invited Laura to go with her to a United Way committee charged with deciding some funding for family and youth programs. The trust that Beki and the committee placed in Laura—to offer great ideas, to be a dependable contributor—helped me see my daughter in a new light and gave Laura a boost in confidence during a hard time. The committee liked what Laura had to say so much that they invited her to become a full-fledged member!

• • • • •

You can help a young friend understand that a person who is lied to no longer trusts the one who lied, and that trust takes time to rebuild—in fact, it has to be earned back. Encouraging truth telling and suggesting a consideration of possible amends to make can facilitate the trust building.

Clarke 1999

44

Go to a Meeting Together

As you get to know young people around you, you'll probably begin to notice issues that have an impact on their lives or that matter a great deal to them—neighborhood safety, the quality of schools, curfews, lack of places to "hang out," environmental concerns.

If you decide that you want first-hand information, go to a public hearing, rally, or candidate debate. And bring along a young person. You won't feel so alone, and your friend is bound to soak up a lesson in civics unlike what he gets from a textbook.

If there's a chance for public comment, encourage your friend to participate. You may have to be brave yourself and go first! Step up to the microphone and speak out on behalf of young people—even if you feel your face flush, knees shake, or palms get sweaty. You'll be a hero to your young pal—and you may even inspire him to do the same.

Keep in mind the words 17-year-old Becky Jarvis of St. Paul, Minnesota, used to promote youth leadership at a 1998 conference of asset builders: "As a youth representative (of Minnesota Alliance with Youth), it is empowering to see adults and their organizations making solid investments in my future and also in my present. But it is even more empowering to work with adults to make that investment in myself."

• • • • •

Youth who thrive feel empowered. Adults empower youth by making sure that they have a chance to add their voices to decisions that affect them and that they have opportunities to define and act on the priorities in their lives.

Scales and Leffert 1999

45

Discuss Your Faith

Perhaps you've held strong faith beliefs all your life. Maybe you're exploring, even challenging, certain beliefs that you grew up with. Perhaps you belong to a faith community or congregation, or maybe you prefer a more solitary form of worship or a quiet, private spirituality.

Wherever you are in your spiritual life, your views are likely to be of great interest to your young friend. Talking about religion and politics may have been widely considered taboo in the past—and in some circumstances it still is—but today most adults believe it's important to discuss personal values with young people. Some ways to get the conversation started are:

- *Tell each other about a favorite holiday or holy day of your faith tradition.*

- *Go to each other's congregation, then talk about what's similar and what's different.*

- *Share your thoughts about prayer or meditation. Do you believe that prayers make a difference?*

- Write down an inspiring quote from sacred scriptures of your faith tradition or from people who share your spiritual beliefs. Trade the quotes, think about them for a couple days, then get together and talk about them.

- Pick a time when your beliefs helped you get through a hard time, then share that story.

• • • • •

Typically, there's a mass exodus of youth from religious involvement between 7th and 9th grade, yet synagogues, churches, mosques, and temples can offer many resources to young people: intergenerational community, opportunities to serve and contribute to community, clear beliefs and values, and a safe place to be themselves and form positive relationships with peers and adults.

Roehlkepartain 1998

46

Plan a Small Event Together

Nothing brings people together quite like food, even if it's just a big bowl of fresh popcorn, and fun. Hook up with your young friend to organize a simple event in your neighborhood, like a soul food potluck, pumpkin carving, holiday cookie exchange, or a video night in your apartment complex or community center. If you're feeling energetic, consider connecting your event to a national day like Neighborhood Night Out (first Tuesday in August) or Make a Difference Day (fourth Saturday in October). In Canada, National Family Week is a great choice for celebrating (the week just prior to Canadian Thanksgiving, the first Monday in October).

If you want to have an outdoor event and the weather's nice, try a neighborhood invitational sports night, with lots of young and older folks involved in sports they can play together, including simple ones like kickball, road hockey, and playing catch. Or how about a music "potluck" or "kitchen party," with neighbors bringing instruments and voices to play music together? Whatever you do, work along with your young friend to make sure people who don't know one another are introduced and welcomed into the fun.

The more familiar your neighbors are with each other, the friendlier and safer the area becomes. And the easier it is for other adults to get to know, rely upon, and enjoy the company of young people they live near.

• • • • •

Neighborhoods most marked by social cohesion (social trust and engagement) are the most effective at reducing neighborhood violence.

Sampson, Raudenbusch, and Earls 1997

47

Review a Resume

Putting together a resume is a little like writing a song—about yourself. With precious few words, it must capture someone's attention and sing your praises. It requires that you look at yourself honestly *and* positively at the same time so that others can see your value.

That's hard enough for adults. And if you're still trying to sort out who you are for your *own* benefit (as many young people are in the midst of doing), writing a resume can seem like mission impossible. But meaningful jobs require resumes, not just applications. And if your young friend is going to learn new skills, be challenged, and make more money, he or she will need a resume.

Encourage your friend to discover his or her "hidden" skills and qualities. Ask: "What's an accomplishment you're most proud of?" Taking charge of a household task when a parent got sick, for example, shows *initiative, responsibility, resourcefulness.* Directing a high school play reflects *leadership skills, an ability to work with people, planning skills.* Pulling out of a downward slide in grades indicates *maturity, discipline, and perseverance.*

While your young friend may not have a long history of employment, with your help he or she can uncover and package his or her gifts and strengths in a way that will get noticed.

• • • • •

In addition to clear vocational goals, work experience, and accurate information, young people must also develop positive personal traits and attitudes, including an optimistic disposition, an internal sense of control, and self-esteem, if they are to make a smooth transition into productive adulthood.

Csikszentmihalyi and Schneider 2000

48

Forgive

Let's say you've worked hard to build a relationship with a young person. Sooner or later, he or she is going to do something that upsets you. It could be almost anything: forgetting to help you with a project, blurting out an offensive comment, ignoring your advice, or even lying or betraying a confidence.

Such upsets happen in any human relationship, and their causes range from little "tests" to misunderstandings to intentional meanness. But strong friendships get past them. Friends eventually forgive each other, no matter what the age difference.

So if you find yourself brooding or angry about something that happened between you two, take a time-out to walk, call another friend, write in your journal, go to a movie, listen to music, mediate, exercise, or say a prayer. When you've gained some perspective on the situation, remind yourself how much he needs adult friends in his life. Talk it over first—remember that without a clarifying conversation, the young person may not know what he did to upset you. Then forgive him. It's fair to expect an "I'm sorry," though it may or may not come right away.

Try to model the concept of forgiving because chances are, you're going to need a little at some point yourself.

• • • • •

A University of Chicago manual prepared for mentors points out that standing by your young friend even when he or she "tests" you sends a very powerful message that your young friend is worth something and that you care enough about him or her to be there.

Freedman 1993

49

Help with Decision Making

Some people seem to reach decisions in a heartbeat, while others virtually wrestle with them.

How does your young friend handle the process? Does she see things only as black-or-white choices? Or does she ponder endlessly, taking too long to decide for fear of making the *wrong* decision?

Either way, your friend can learn from how *you* make decisions. Do you:

- *Make a list of pros and cons, then see which is longer or has more "weight"?*

- *Set a time limit for mulling, then go with your "gut" feeling?*

- *Create mental scenarios of the results of possible choices?*

- *Check in with a few trusted friends to get their opinions?*

- *Write down all your questions about the decision, then seek more information?*

Has the way you make decisions changed over time, as you piled up more experiences from which to draw or gained maturity?

Young people face a raft of decisions: What classes should they take? How do they handle pressures about substance use, sexual activity, relationships? What will they do when high school is out for summer? Over for good? It's their job to sort out the questions, but you can help by showing them how to make decisions wisely.

• • • • •

Teens achieve or are capable of achieving the capacities for critical thinking and competent decision making by early to middle adolescence.

Keating 1990

50

Be a Rock

I heard this story at a Catholic mass one Sunday and have never forgotten it!

After a nasty fight with her mother, a 15-year-old girl slammed the door to her bedroom, cried herself into exhaustion, and didn't come out of her room for the rest of the night.

The next morning, when she opened her bedroom door, she found a little box on the floor just outside her room. She picked it up, plopped herself on the bed, and opened the small package. Inside she found a rock wrapped in a piece of paper on which were written 20 words.

It took less than a minute to read the message, but she'll have a lifetime to bask in its meaning. She practically flew to her mom and wrapped her in a bear hug.

The words on the note: *"This rock is 30 million years old. That's how long it will be before I ever give up on you."*

Do you know someone who could use a rock?

• • • • •

The work of many researchers has shown over the past two decades that resilient youth have at least one adult who cares deeply for them. Psychologist Urie Bronfenbrenner said that all children need someone in their lives who is simply "crazy" about them.

Bronfenbrenner 1991

SOURCES
and Resources

BIBLIOGRAPHY OF RESEARCH SOURCES

page 15 Schorr, L. B. (1997). *Common purpose: Strengthening families and neighborhoods to rebuild America.* New York: Anchor Books/Doubleday, p. 307.

page 17 Page, R. M. (1992). Feelings of physical unattractiveness and hopelessness among high school students. *High School Journal, 75,* 150–155.

page 19 Scales, P. C., & Leffert, N. (1999). *Developmental assets: A synthesis of the scientific research on adolescent development.* Minneapolis: Search Institute, p. 12.

page 21 Saito, R. N., Sullivan, T. K., & Hintz, N. R. (2000). *The possible dream: What families in distressed communities need to help youth thrive.* Minneapolis: Search Institute, p. 28.

page 23 Scales, P. C., & Leffert, N. (1999). *Developmental assets: A synthesis of the scientific research on adolescent development.* Minneapolis: Search Institute, p. 100.

page 25 Hodgkinson, V. A., & Weitzman, M. S. (with Crutchfield, E. A., & Heffron, A. J.). (1996). *Volunteering and giving among teenagers 12 to 17 years of age.* Washington, DC: Independent Sector.

page 27 Scales, P. C., & Leffert, N. (1999). *Developmental assets: A synthesis of the scientific research on adolescent development.* Minneapolis: Search Institute, p. 27.

page 29 Farkas, S., & Johnson, J. (1997). *Kids these days: What Americans really think of the next generation.* New York: Public Agenda, p. 43.

page 31 Scales, P. C., & Leffert, N. (1999). *Developmental assets: A synthesis of the scientific research on adolescent development.* Minneapolis: Search Institute, pp. 78–79.

page 33 Clarke, J. I. (1999). *Connections: The threads that strengthen families.* Center City, MN: Hazelden, pp. 10–11.

page 35 Stringer, S. A. (1997). *Conflict and connection: The psychology of young adult literature.* Portsmouth, NH: Boynton/Cook Publishers, p. 89.

page 37 Carnegie Council on Adolescent Development. (1995). *Great transitions: Preparing adolescents for a new century.* New York: Carnegie Council of New York, p. 21.

page 39 Scales, P.C., & Leffert, N. (1999). *Developmental Assets: A synthesis of the scientific research on adolescent development.* Minneapolis: Search Institute, p. 53.

page 41 Starkman, N., Scales, P. C., & Roberts, C. (1999). *Great places to learn: How asset-building schools help students succeed.* Minneapolis: Search Institute, pp. 45–46.

page 43 Elliott, D.S., Wilson, W. J., Huizinga, D., Sampson, R. J., Elliott, A., & Rankin, B. (1996). The effects of neighborhood disadvantage on adolescent development. *Journal of Research in Crime and Delinquency, 33,* 389–426.

page 45 Scales, P. C. (2001). The public image of adolescents. *Society 38*(4), 65.

page 47 Beardsley, D. A. (1982). Social values, interpersonal relationships, bibliotherapy, and the social studies. Springfield, MO: Southwest Missouri State University. (ERIC Document Reproduction Service No. ED227048).

page 49 Hodgkinson, V. A., & Weitzman, M. S. (with Crutchfield, E. A., & Heffron, A. J.). (1996). *Volunteering and giving among teenagers 12 to 17 years of age.* Washington, DC: Independent Sector.

page 51 Seligman, Martin E. P. (1998). *Learned optimism: How to change your mind and your life.* New York: Pocket Books.

page 53 Scales, P. C., & Leffert, N. (1999). *Developmental assets: A synthesis of the scientific research on adolescent development.* Minneapolis: Search Institute, p. 159

page 54 Sultanoff, S. M. (1999). Where has all my humor gone; long time passing . . . humor from children to adults. Originally published as the president's column in *Therapeutic Humor, 18*(4), 2. (found online on April 10, 2002, at www.humormatters.com/articles/growingserious.htm).

page 55 Scales, P. C., Benson, P. L., & Roehlkepartain, E. C. (2001). *Grading grown-ups: American adults report on their real relationships with kids.* Minneapolis: Lutheran Brotherhood and Search Institute, p. 32.

page 57 Carnegie Council on Adolescent Development (1995). *Great transitions: Preparing adolescents for a new century.* New York: Carnegie Corporation of New York, p. 21.

page 59 Hipp, E. (1991). *Feed your head: Some excellent stuff on being yourself.* Center City, MN: Hazelden, p. 65.

page 61 Saito, R.N., Sullivan, T.K., & Hintz, N.R. *The possible dream: What families in distressed communities need to help youth thrive.* Minneapolis: Search Institute, p. 5.

page 63 Scales, P.C., & Leffert, N. (1999). *Developmental assets: A synthesis of the scientific research on adolescent development* (Minneapolis: Search Institute, 1999), p. 89.

page 65   Kraehmer, S. T. (1995). *Heroes: Shaping lives through family and culture.* Minneapolis: Fairview Press, p. 4.

page 67   Stringer, S. A. (1997). *Conflict and connection: The psychology of young adult literature.* Portsmouth, NH:Boynton/Cook Publishers, pp. 16–17.

page 69   Damon, W. (1988). *The moral child: Nurturing children's natural moral growth.* New York: Free Press, p. 119.

page 71   Csikszentmihalyi, M., & Schneider, B. (2000). *Becoming adult: How teenagers prepare for the world of work.* New York: Basic Books, p. 72–73.

page 73   Carnegie Council on Adolescent Development. (1995). *Great transitions: Preparing adolescents for a new century.* New York: Carnegie Corporation of New York, p. 110.

page 75   Scales, P. C., & Gibbons, J. L. (1996). Extended family members and unrelated adults in the lives of young adolescents: A research agenda. *Journal of Early Adolescence, 16,* 365–89.

page 77   Talmi, A., & Harter, S. (1998). *Pathways to better outcomes: Special adults as sources of support for young adolescents.* Paper presented at the biennial meetings of the Society for Research on Adolescence, San Diego, CA.

page 79   Scales, P. C., Benson, P. L., & Roehlkepartain, E. C. (2001). *Grading grown-ups: American adults report on their real relationships with kids.* Minneapolis: Lutheran Brotherhood and Search Institute, p. 14.

      The full story of Joan Baez and Ira can be found in Madigan, C. O., & Elwood, A. (1998), *When they were kids: Over 400 sketches of famous childhoods.* New York: Random House, p. 184.

page 81   Stringer, S. A. (1997). *Conflict and connection: The psychology of young adult literature.* Portsmouth, NH: Boynton/Cook Publishers, p. 62.

page 83   Weeks, D. (1994). *The eight essential steps to conflict resolution: Preserving relationships at work, at home, and in the community.* New York: Putnam, p. 8.

page 85   Godfrey, N. S. (1995). *A penny saved: Teaching your children the values and life skills they will need to live in the real world.* New York: Simon & Schuster, p. 17.

page 87   Scales, P. C., Benson, P. L., & Roehlkepartain, E. C. (2001). *Grading grown-ups: American adults report on their real relationships with kids.* Minneapolis: Lutheran Brotherhood and Search Institute, p. 14.

page 89   Torney-Purta, J., Lehmann, R., Oswald, H., & Schulz, W. (2001). *Citizenship and education in twenty-eight countries: Civic knowledge and engagement at age 14.* Amsterdam: International Association for the Evaluation of Educational Achievement.

page 91   Csikszentmihalyi, M., & Schneider, B. (2000). *Becoming adult: How teenagers prepare for the world of work.* New York: Basic Books, p. 14.

page 93   Scales, P. C., Benson, P. L., & Roehlkepartain, E. C. (2001). *Grading grown-ups: American adults report on their real relationships with kids.* Minneapolis; Lutheran Brotherhood and Search Institute, p. 11.

page 95   Hersch, P. (1998). *A tribe apart: A journey into the heart of American adolescence.* New York: Fawcett Columbine, p. 372.

page 97   Clarke, J. I. (1999). *Connections: The threads that strengthen families.* Center City, MN: Hazelden, p. 97.

page 99   Scales, P. C., & Leffert, N. (1999). *Developmental assets: A synthesis of the scientific research on adolescent development.* Minneapolis: Search Institute, p. 51.

page 101   Roehlkepartain, E. C. (1998). *Building assets in congregations: A practical guide for helping youth grow up healthy.* Minneapolis: Search Institute, p. xiii.

page 103   Sampson, R. J., Raudenbusch, S. W., & Earls, F. (1997). Neighborhoods and violent crime: A multilevel study of collective efficacy. *Science, 277,* 918-24.

page 105   Csikszentmihalyi, M., & Schneider, B. (2000). *Becoming adult: How teenagers prepare for the world of work.* New York: Basic Books, p. 221.

page 107   Freedman, M. (1993). *The kindness of strangers: Adult mentors, urban youth, and the new volunteerism.* San Francisco: Jossey-Bass, p. 102.

page 109   Keating, D.P. (1990). Adolescent thinking. In S. S. Feldman & G. R. Elliott (Eds.), *At the threshold: The developing adolescent* (pp. 54-92). Cambridge, MA: Harvard University Press.

page 111   Bronfenbrenner, U. (1991). Sources of competence and character: What do families do? *Family Affairs, 4* (1-2), 1-6.

-or-

What to remember when that little voice inside says that maybe you don't have what it takes to connect with a young person

I'm not a professional youth worker.

Not a problem. Young people need all kinds of adults in their lives, not just those who've studied youth development or who've made a career out of working with adolescents. And they're not so complicated that you need a special degree to understand them. They're human, just like you. They need neighbors who know their names, adult friends who send them cards of encouragement or attend their recitals, games, or plays, and coworkers and employers who value their opinions and teach them new skills. No matter how big or small, every effort you make to get to know young people builds part of a powerful web of support for them. (Just so you know, one of the young people who reviewed this book says his parents are youth workers, and he rather likes having adults in his life who don't know so much about youth!)

2

Won't young people and their parents be leery of a stranger like me trying to be a friend?

It's possible. And of course, many young people are taught to beware of all strangers. We're not suggesting you burst into someone's home and announce, "Here I am, your brand-new friend!" What we're encouraging you to do is realize how much young people need caring, supportive adults in their lives beyond their homes and schools and to look for and seize the small opportunities that arise daily. We hope that you will be open to new friendships and get acquainted in a respectful way and at a comfortable pace. Safe public areas—parks, restaurants, coffee shops, grocery stores, schools—are good places to foster friendships, build trust, and connect with others. Once you get to know a young person, encourage your new friend to let her or his parents know about your activities together, and, if possible, introduce yourself to her or his parents or guardian.

If this is a particular concern for you, try talking with a friend who's a parent about getting more involved in her or his child's life. Maybe your friend could invite you to go along to a school concert or other event, or you could offer to spend a fun afternoon with the child while your friend runs errands.

It's the parents' job, not mine, to raise kids.

You're right—mostly. Their job is to be a parent. But consider the words of a wise 16-year-old who was counseling a friend. The friend's little brother was drinking, running away, and skipping school and she said her mother felt like the worst parent in the world. "Tell your mother this," the teen said to her friend. "Tell your mother that parents aren't the only ones who raise kids. Teachers raise kids. Kids raise kids. Neighbors raise kids. Everyone's raising kids. Your mother shouldn't have to feel so all alone." Truth is, parenting is a tough job even though it's a rewarding one. Think how great it would be for parents to have some help now and then from another adult; after all, young people can't get too much support. And remember, no parent or guardian alone can be everything to a child, especially as he or she grows up. And sometimes another adult can talk with a child about schoolwork or the future or their current lifestyle or behavior in a way that gets through to the child better.

Young people's problems are so complex; there's nothing I can do.

Remember, you *have* an impact on young people even if you *don't* interact with them—through role modeling, or through not paying attention to them, for example—but you're more likely to have a positive impact if you try to be an intentional asset builder. Besides, not all young people are struggling with mega-problems. You can be sure, though, that a fair number are lonely and could benefit from the friendship of some caring adults. In one study by the World Health Organization during the 1997–1998 school year, nearly 20% of 15-year-olds from the U.S. reported feeling lonely.

And think about it for a minute—put yourself in a teen's shoes. Even if you were a teen who was coping with depression, substance abuse, or an eating disorder and even if you saw a raft of specialists for these problems or were on probation for something, you would still need adult friends in your life, right? You'd still need people with whom you could bounce ideas, go to a movie, laugh over an embarrassing moment, or talk with about future plans. So, try not to think of yourself as a problem-fixer. Consider yourself a friend—that's all, and that's plenty.

Teenagers and I are too different to be friends.

If you feel intimidated by the "cultural" gaps in the modern world—differences that arise from race, age, generation, language, ability, education level, wealth—imagine what it's like for someone who's barely into his or her second decade of life.

Remember that you and the teenager are both strangers to one another at first; he or she may be feeling a little awkward or uncomfortable, too. But if you take a second look at this situation, maybe you'll be comforted by the idea that that discomfort is something you and the young person have in common.

Realize that you're both starting from the same place, but as an adult you have the benefit of a few extra years of experience, and maybe more confidence. Look beyond the surface. Allow yourself to be curious and to learn. Don't think you have to be an expert in the latest music, lingo, clothes, or piercing trends to make a connection with a young person. In fact, that's not what most young people want; they want you to be a grown-up, but a grown-up who connects with them and looks for common ground with them. You don't have to be the same as one another; but as you explore similarities and differences, your mutual understanding will fill the gaps and maybe even form a friendship bond that lasts.

I don't cross paths with youth much. How can I possibly connect with them?

For one day, pay extra close attention to who crosses your path. My guess is that you probably do encounter young people more than you realize. How about the grocery store?

Or the gas station? Or the shopping mall? Even small connections, like smiling, are a good start. But you can go further. Do you have friends or coworkers who are parents? Ask if they would like you to spend some time with one or more of their children. Stop by a community center, local school, or your congregation and ask what opportunities they have available or activities that might interest you. If you're in an assisted living apartment or a nursing home, ask the aides or nurses if they have children who could use an older friend in their lives. Once you take the first step, you'll be amazed how many options open up to cross paths with young people.

I'll be rejected. I'm not exactly "cool," you know.

One young person who reviewed an earlier draft of this book told me this: "If you try too hard to be 'cool,' young people will be able to tell and it will make you look bad in their eyes." So don't worry: Most young people don't exactly *expect* you to be cool. What's more important to them is that you be authentic. They'd much rather you *be yourself,* complete with all your quirks and imperfections, than keep your distance for fear of being uncool. If you can show sincere interest in young people as unique human beings with gifts to be discovered—as people who deserve to be respected and supported— that's really all it takes. So, in the words of several young people who contributed ideas to this book: "Be you." You'll be surprised how fast you connect with young people when you genuinely take an interest in who they are.

Teens just want their independence. They don't like adults and don't really want us around.

Some teens *are* incredibly independent and competent. And that's good; those qualities will help them grow into strong and happy adults. But most young people still need a safety net of support and affirmation as they try to do more things on their own. It's a rare teen who doesn't look to some adult as an example of how to make a living, solve a problem, take a stand, or mend a relationship. Especially while young people explore their identity and try to gain some independence from their parents, they need other caring adults to encourage them, cheer them on, challenge them, make them think, teach them skills, and show them new points of view. It's true that young people don't like *certain* adults—those who dismiss their opinions, expect the worst of them, patronize them, belittle them, treat them unfairly, or fail to see their gifts. Most teens thrive when they're recognized by adults and treated with respect. Neither is hard to do. We show you lots of ways in this book.

The developmental assets are spread across eight broad areas of human development. These categories paint a picture of the positive things all young people need to grow up healthy and responsible. The first four asset categories focus on external structures, relationships, and activities that create a positive environment for young people:

 Support—Young people need to be surrounded by people who love, care for, appreciate, and accept them. They need to know that they belong and that they are not alone.

 Empowerment—Young people need to feel valued and valuable. This happens when youth feel safe, when they believe that they are liked and respected, and when they contribute to their families and communities.

 Boundaries and Expectations—Young people need the positive influence of peers and adults who encourage them to be and do their best. Youth also need clear rules about appropriate behavior, and consistent, reasonable consequences for breaking those rules.

Constructive Use of Time—Young people need opportunities—outside of school—to learn and develop new skills and interests, and to spend enjoyable time interacting with other youth and adults.

The next four categories reflect internal values, skills, and beliefs that young people also need to develop to fully engage with and function in the world around them:

 Commitment to Learning—Young people need a variety of learning experiences, including the desire for academic success, a sense of the lasting importance of learning, and a belief in their own abilities.

 Positive Values—Young people need to develop strong guiding values or principles, including caring about others, having high standards for personal character, and believing in protecting their own well-being.

 Social Competencies—Young people need to develop the skills to interact effectively with others, to make difficult decisions and choices, and to cope with new situations.

Positive Identity—Young people need to believe in their own self-worth, to feel that they have control over the things that happen to them, and to have a sense of purpose in life as well as a positive view of the future.

The Challenge

The good news is that the assets are powerful and that everyone can build them (we call intentionally trying to help youth develop these strengths *building assets*). The challenge for all of us is that most young people aren't experiencing enough of them. While there is no "magic number" of assets young people should have, our data indicate that 31 is a worthy, though challenging, benchmark for experiencing their positive effects most strongly. Yet, as this chart shows, only 9 percent of surveyed youth report having 31 or more assets. More than half have 20 or fewer assets.

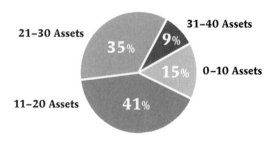

On the next pages, you'll find a complete chart of the developmental assets in English and in Spanish.

Search Institute has identified the following building blocks of healthy development that help young people grow up healthy, caring, and responsible.

EXTERNAL ASSETS

SUPPORT

1. **Family support**—Family life provides high levels of love and support.

2. **Positive family communication**—Young person and her or his parent(s) communicate positively, and young person is willing to seek advice and counsel from parents.

3. **Other adult relationships**—Young person receives support from three or more nonparent adults.

4. **Caring neighborhood**—Young person experiences caring neighbors.

5. **Caring school climate**—School provides a caring, encouraging environment.

6. **Parent involvement in schooling**—Parent(s) are actively involved in helping young person succeed in school.

EMPOWERMENT

7. **Community values youth**—Young person perceives that adults in the community value youth.

8. **Youth as resources**—Young people are given useful roles in the community.

9. **Service to others**—Young person serves in the community one hour or more per week.

10. **Safety**—Young person feels safe at home, at school, and in the neighborhood.

EXTERNAL ASSETS

BOUNDARIES AND EXPECTATIONS

11. **Family boundaries**—Family has clear rules and consequences and monitors the young person's whereabouts.

12. **School boundaries**—School provides clear rules and consequences.

13. **Neighborhood boundaries**—Neighbors take responsibility for monitoring young people's behavior.

14. **Adult role models**—Parent(s) and other adults model positive, responsible behavior.

15. **Positive peer influence**—Young person's best friends model responsible behavior.

16. **High expectations**—Both parent(s) and teachers encourage the young person to do well.

CONSTRUCTIVE USE OF TIME

17. **Creative activities**—Young person spends three or more hours per week in lessons or practice in music, theater, or other arts.

18. **Youth programs**—Young person spends three or more hours per week in sports, clubs, or organizations at school and/or in the community.

19. **Religious community**—Young person spends one or more hours per week in activities in a religious institution.

20. **Time at home**—Young person is out with friends "with nothing special to do" two or fewer nights per week.

INTERNAL ASSETS

COMMITMENT TO LEARNING

21. Achievement motivation—Young person is motivated to do well in school.

22. School engagement—Young person is actively engaged in learning.

23. Homework—Young person reports doing at least one hour of homework every school day.

24. Bonding to school—Young person cares about her or his school.

25. Reading for pleasure—Young person reads for pleasure three or more hours per week.

POSITIVE VALUES

26. Caring—Young person places high value on helping other people.

27. Equality and social justice—Young person places high value on promoting equality and reducing hunger and poverty.

28. Integrity—Young person acts on convictions and stands up for her or his beliefs.

29. Honesty—Young person "tells the truth even when it is not easy."

30. Responsibility—Young person accepts and takes personal responsibility.

31. Restraint—Young person believes it is important not to be sexually active or to use alcohol or other drugs.

INTERNAL ASSETS

SOCIAL COMPETENCIES

32. Planning and decision making—Young person knows how to plan ahead and make choices.

33. Interpersonal competence—Young person has empathy, sensitivity, and friendship skills.

34. Cultural competence—Young person has knowledge of and comfort with people of different cultural/racial/ethnic backgrounds.

35. Resistance skills—Young person can resist negative peer pressure and dangerous situations.

36. Peaceful conflict resolution—Young person seeks to resolve conflict nonviolently.

POSITIVE IDENTITY

37. Personal power—Young person feels he or she has control over "things that happen to me."

38. Self-esteem—Young person reports having a high self-esteem.

39. Sense of purpose—Young person reports that "my life has a purpose."

40. Positive view of personal future—Young person is optimistic about her or his personal future.

La investigación realizada por el Instituto Search ha identificado los siguientes elementos fundamentales del desarrollo como instrumentos para ayudar a los jóvenes a crecer sanos, interesados en el bienestar común y a ser responsables.

ELEMENTOS FUNDAMENTALES EXTERNOS

APOYO

1. **Apoyo familiar**—La vida familiar brinda altos niveles de amor y apoyo.

2. **Comunicación familiar positiva**—El (La) joven y sus padres se comunican positivamente. Los jóvenes están dispuestos a buscar consejo y consuelo en sus padres.

3. **Otras relaciones con adultos**—Además de sus padres, los jóvenes reciben apoyo de tres o más personas adultas que no son sus parientes.

4. **Una comunidad comprometida**—El (La) joven experimenta el interés de sus vecinos por su bienestar.

5. **Un plantel educativo que se interesa por el (la) joven**—La escuela proporciona un ambiente que anima y se preocupa por la juventud.

6. **La participación de los padres en las actividades escolares**—Los padres participan activamente ayudando a los jóvenes a tener éxito en la escuela.

FORTALECIMIENTO

7. **La comunidad valora a la juventud**—El (La) joven percibe que los adultos en la comunidad valoran a la juventud.

8. **La juventud como un recurso**—Se le brinda a los jóvenes la oportunidad de tomar un papel útil en la comunidad.

9. **Servicio a los demás**—La gente joven participa brindando servicios a su comunidad una hora o más a la semana.

10. **Seguridad**—Los jóvenes se sienten seguros en casa, en la escuela y en el vecindario.

ELEMENTOS FUNDAMENTALES EXTERNOS

LÍMITES Y EXPECTATIVAS

11. Límites familiares—La familia tiene reglas y consecuencias bien claras, además vigila las actividades de los jóvenes.

12. Límites escolares—En la escuela proporciona reglas y consecuencias bien claras.

13. Límites vecinales—Los vecinos asumen la responsabilidad de vigilar el comportamiento de los jóvenes.

14. El comportamiento de los adultos como ejemplo—Los padres y otros adultos tienen un comportamiento positivo y responsable.

15. Compañeros como influencia positiva—Los mejores amigos del (la) joven son un buen ejemplo de comportamiento responsable.

16. Altas expectativas—Ambos padres y maestros motivan a los jóvenes para que tengan éxito.

USO CONSTRUCTIVO DEL TIEMPO

17. Actividades creativas—Los jóvenes pasan tres horas o más a la semana en lecciones de música, teatro u otras artes.

18. Programas juveniles—Los jóvenes pasan tres horas o más a la semana practicando algún deporte, o en organizaciones en la escuela o de la comunidad.

19. Comunidad religiosa—Los jóvenes pasan una hora o más a la semana en actividades organizadas por alguna institución religiosa.

20. Tiempo en casa—Los jóvenes conviven con sus amigos "sin nada especial que hacer" dos o pocas noches por semana.

ELEMENTOS FUNDAMENTALES INTERNOS

COMPROMISO CON EL APRENDIZAJE

21. Motivación por sus logros—El (La) joven es motivado(a) para que salga bien en la escuela.

22. Compromiso con la escuela—El (La) joven participa activamente con el aprendizaje.

23. Tarea—El (La) joven debe hacer su tarea escolar por lo menos durante una hora cada día de clases.

24. Preocuparse por la escuela—Al (A la) joven debe importarle su escuela.

25. Leer por placer—El (La) joven lee por placer tres horas o más por semana.

VALORES POSITIVOS

26. Preocuparse por los demás—El (La) joven valora ayudar a los demás.

27. Igualdad y justicia social—Para el (la) joven tiene mucho valor el promover la igualdad y reducir el hambre y la pobreza.

28. Integridad—El (La) joven actúa con convicción y defiende sus creencias.

29. Honestidad—El (La) joven "dice la verdad aún cuando esto no sea fácil".

30. Responsabilidad—El (La) joven acepta y toma responsabilidad por su persona.

31. Abstinencia—El (La) joven cree que es importante no estar activo(a) sexualmente, ni usar alcohol u otras drogas.

Elementos Fundamentales Internos

CAPACIDAD SOCIAL

32. Planeación y toma de decisiones—El (La) joven sabe cómo planear y hacer elecciones.

33. Capacidad interpersonal—El (La) joven es sympático, sensible y hábil para hacer amistades.

34. Capacidad cultural—El (La) joven tiene conocimiento de y sabe convivir con gente de diferente marco cultural, racial o étnico.

35. Habilidad de resistencia—El (La) joven puede resistir la presión negativa de los compañeros así como las situaciones peligrosas.

36. Solución pacífica de conflictos—El (La) joven busca resolver los conflictos sin violencia.

IDENTIDAD POSITIVA

37. Poder personal—El (La) joven siente que él o ella tiene el control de "las cosas que le suceden".

38. Auto-estima—El (La) joven afirma tener una alta auto-estima.

39. Sentido de propósito—El (La) joven afirma que "mi vida tiene un propósito".

40. Visión positiva del futuro personal—El (La) joven es optimista sobre su futuro mismo.

ADDITIONAL SEARCH INSTITUTE RESOURCES

Want to learn more about the developmental assets and how to use them? Take a look at these resources available from Search Institute through our Web site at www.search-institute.org. And check out our online catalog for even more videos, books, posters, and workbooks.

• • • • •

Tag, You're It! poster. This colorful new two-poster handout complements the *Tag, You're It!* book. The poster is perforated in the middle, with one side for young people and one side for adults. Young people and adults alike can use them to hang up side by side, as reminders of what we all have in common, or tear them apart and give one away as an invitation to start a healthy intergenerational relationship. In sets of 20.

• • • • •

Assets Happening Here video. Produced by teens for teens and centered on the real lives of three young people, this video focuses on what it takes for young people to grow up healthy, caring, and responsible by centering on the real lives of three diverse teens. Produced by Noodle-Head Network.

• • • • •

Building Assets Together: 135 Group Activities for Helping Youth Succeed. Designed to help young people examine each of the developmental assets, this book includes experiential activities and creative worksheets on each of the 40 assets. Many activities can easily be incorporated into various organizations' regular youth activities.

• • • • •

In Good Company: Tools to Help Youth and Adults Talk. This 48-page workbook includes a quick introduction, get-acquainted activities, and perforated tear-out sheets for eight guided conversations for youth-adult pairs, one on each asset category.

• • • • •

In Our Own Words Posters. This set of eight eye-catching posters was inspired and written by young people, featuring phrases and words that 17 young people used to describe what an asset category means to them.

• • • • •

Step by Step! A Young Person's Guide to Positive Community Change. To quote the young people who co-wrote this guide, "You don't have to be famous or brilliant or rich to make a difference. You just have to care and then do something about it." They provide the ideas and tools for other young people to make change in their community, including how to involve adults to help, and share the tips and trials of their own work to get a new community center built in their own neighborhood.

• • • • •

Taking Asset Building Personally: Planning Guide and Personal Action Workbook. With the planning and discussion guide plus six copies of the Action and Reflection workbook, you'll have everything you need to work in a small group on making the assets a part of your neighborhood group or book club members' lives. Fun, thought-provoking, and filled with ideas and information.